FLASHBACKS

THE FLASHBACKS SERIES IS SPONSORED BY THE
EUROPEAN ETHNOLOGICAL RESEARCH CENTRE
CELTIC & SCOTTISH STUDIES
UNIVERSITY OF EDINBURGH
27-29 GEORGE STREET
EDINBURGH EH8 9LD

FLASHBACKS

FLASHBACKS

Scotland's Land Girls

Breeches, Bombers and Backaches

Edited by
Elaine M. Edwards

in association with
THE EUROPEAN ETHNOLOGICAL RESEARCH CENTRE
AND NMS ENTERPRISES LIMITED – PUBLISHING
NATIONAL MUSEUMS SCOTLAND

GENERAL EDITOR
Alexander Fenton

Published in Great Britain in 2010 by
NMS Enterprises Limited – Publishing
NMS Enterprises Limited
National Museums Scotland
Chambers Street, Edinburgh EH1 1JF

ISBN 978-1-905267-32-3

**British Library Cataloguing in
Publication Data**
A catalogue record of this book
is available from the British Library.

Cover design by Mark Blackadder.
Cover photograph:
  Margaret Watson (*née* Macbeth)
  (right) wearing WLA dungarees,
  taking a well-earned break with
  her sister, *c*1948, Lanarkshire.
  (*Source:* Margaret Watson)
Internal text design by NMS Enter-
  prises Limited – Publishing.
Printed and bound in Great Britain by
  Bell & Bain Limited, Glasgow.

For a full listing of related NMS
titles please visit:

www.nms.ac.uk/books

CONTENTS

ACKNOWLEDGEMENTS

THIS book was conceived and shaped in discussions with Mark Mulhern of the European Ethnological Research Centre and Lesley Taylor at National Museums Scotland. John Burnett (National Museums Scotland) and Mark Mulhern assisted with the preparation of the final text, and to them I wish to express special thanks. Others helped by advising on specific points or by checking the text: Kate Mackay, Duncan Dornan, Marion Lawton, Bob Powell, Dorothy O'Neill, and I am grateful to them all. I am, of course, responsible for any errors that remain.

Elaine M. Edwards

LIST OF ILLUSTRATIONS

MAIN TEXT

page 13. Auchincruive House, from the Thomas Annan Collections. (Reproduced by permission of The Mitchell Library)

page 14. Recruiting poster for the Women's Land Army produced as part of the 'Lend a hand on the land' campaign. National Archives, INF 13/140 (19). (*Source:* National Archives of Scotland)

ART SECTION

1. Jean Forbes Paterson being taught to shear with hand-clippers, *c*1946, Perthshire. (*Source:* Jean Forbes Paterson)
2. (a) and (b): Women's Land Army membership card belonging to Jean Forbes Paterson. (*Source:* Jean Forbes Paterson)
3. Jean Forbes Paterson (far left) with pals on a Fordson tractor, *c*1946, Perthshire. (*Source:* Jean Forbes Paterson)
4. Wartime Identity Card belonging to Jean Forbes Paterson. (*Source:* Jean Forbes Paterson)
5. Ellanora Sherry (*née* McLaughlin) (far left), on a day off from her Land Army work, *c*1943, Lanark. (*Source:* Ellanora Sherry)
6. Ellanora Sherry (*née* McLaughlin) (front right), *c*1943, Lanark. (*Source:* Ellanora Sherry)
7. Elizabeth (Betty) Lowe (*née* Wyllie), *c*1943, Craigeassie, Angus. (*Source:* Elizabeth Lowe)
8. Una Stewart (*née* Marshall) using an evacuated milking system, *c*1943, Angus. (*Source:* Una Stewart)
9. Una Stewart (*née* Marshall) helping a calf to feed from a bucket, *c*1943, Angus. (*Source:* Una Stewart)
10. Marion Allison (*née* MacMillan) in the WLA uniform, *c*1942, at Westerhouse Farm, Carluke, Lanarkshire. (*Source:* Marion Allison)
11. Marion Allison (*née* MacMillan) was joined for a short time by another

Land Girl, Elsie Graham (later Todd), *c*1943, Carluke, Lanarkshire. (*Source:* Marion Allison)

12. Laura Bauld (*née* Lindsay) using a Rotovator, *c*1948, East Lothian. (*Source:* Laura Bauld)

13. Laura Bauld (*née* Lindsay) with her future husband, Willie, at Greenend Farm, *c*1948, East Lothian. (*Source:* Laura Bauld)

14. Laura Bauld (*née* Lindsay) with an unnamed boy, hoeing, *c*1948, East Lothian. (*Source:* Laura Bauld)

15. Anna Searson (*née* Murray) on a trip to the photographer's studio, 21 August 1943, modelling the full WLA uniform, including the hat, Ayrshire. (*Source:* Anna Searson)

16. A studio portrait of Isabella (Isa) Rankin (née Barker) in her Land Army uniform, minus the hat! Taken *c*1942, while serving at Pencaitland, East Lothian. (*Source:* Isabella Rankin)

17. Isabella (Isa) Rankin (*née* Barker) (second left) with colleagues at Dovecot Market Garden, Haddington, *c*1943. (*Source:* Isabella Rankin)

18. Mona McLeod (far right, behind the hedge) at a tea-party organised by Mrs Jessie Grierson, SWLA Representative for Galloway, 1941. Despite having served for nine months, this was the first opportunity Mona had had to meet other Land Girls. (*Source:* Mona McLeod)

19. Mona McLeod (left) with fellow Land Girls, Bobby Stubley and Doris Brown, enjoying a little time off, *c*1941, Solway Firth, Galloway. (*Source:* Mona McLeod)

20. Mona McLeod in her WLA uniform and doing her favourite job as a Land Girl, working with the horses, *c*1942, Galloway. (*Source:* Mona McLeod)

21. Margaret Watson (*née* Macbeth) wearing an old battle-dress jacket, scything, *c*1948, Lanarkshire. (*Source:* Margaret Watson)

22. Margaret Watson (*née* Macbeth) (right) wearing WLA dungarees, taking a well-earned break with her sister, *c*1948, Lanarkshire. (*Source:* Margaret Watson)

23. Petrina (Ina) Lithgow (*née* Seaton) standing (back, right) next to her former school friend Agnes Boyle (*née* Flucker), East Lothian, *c*1943. Ina and Agnes remain close friends to this day. (*Source:* Petrina Lithgow)

EDITORIAL NOTE

THE stories in this book give a flavour of life in the Women's Land Army in Scotland's countryside during World War II. The first two Land Girls I met were Ina Lithgow (*née* Seaton) and Agnes Boyle (*née* Flucker). We met by chance in 2005 at an event to mark the sixtieth anniversary of VE Day. Having an enthusiasm for women's history I was keen to record their experiences for future generations, although at the time I did not envision this resulting in a book. Word of mouth contacts and appeals for former Land Girls to come forward have brought me into contact with many Girls, all of whom have possessed a certain stoicism and zest for life's challenges. Their memories are told many years after the event, and although those who responded to my appeal for information tend to be the ones that enjoyed their time in the Women's Land Army, I believe they still retain a realistic recollection of conditions in the fields and of their daily lives.

Four of the memoirs are in the Girls' own words. The longest, by Jean Forbes Paterson, has been printed at the beginning because it provides a detailed description of farming practice in Scotland in the 1940s, and so introduces the following accounts. The rest of the reminiscences were told to me directly in interviews, letters, and in sound recordings made for the exhibition 'Land Girls and Lumber Jills' held in the National War Museum Scotland (2010-11). The versions presented here are reconstructions from all the information available to me.

I have been most fortunate in forging friendships with a number of Land Girls: they have taken me into their confidence and have welcomed me into their homes. Women are so often in the shadows, especially when history is being recorded. Fortunately this is being addressed as greater interest is taken in the role women played in society. Women are at their best when they forge strong bonds, have a cause to rally to, and show what tenacity and strength they have both physically and mentally. These qualities emerge in what follows.

Elaine M. Edwards
National Museum of Rural Life
WESTER KITTOCHSIDE 2010

FOREWORD

THE 'Flashbacks' series presents, in printed form, the words of individuals concerning aspects of – or the entirety of – their lives in Scotland. The content is variously composed of interview transcriptions, memoir or autobiography. The aim of the series is to gather in fragments of life as it is actually lived, and to re-transmit them to a wider audience.

Individually and collectively, the volumes of the 'Flashbacks' give an account of 'what a life was' in different places. These volumes do this by giving an insight into the ways in which the individual lived and how they felt about that life. By allowing people to give their own account, in their own words, the reader gains an insight into different lives in different parts of Scotland.

This particular volume recounts the experience of wartime service of a number of women. Following on from the earlier title in the series – *Timber!* – which focused on the lives of wartime Lumber Jills in Scotland, this volume reveals the reminiscences and reflections of a number of women who served in the Scottish Women's Land Army. After a long gap there is now growing interest in knowing about, and marking the achievements of, women who served in the Land Army in World Wars I and II. This volume allows the 'Girls' – a term which the women affectionately use to describe themselves – to provide the reader with first-hand insight into an important aspect of their lives: important to them and important to the country they were serving.

The essence of the 'Flashbacks' series is the everyday life of as broad a sample of people as possible – even in unusual circumstances such as wartime. Everyday life is often held to be that which is lived in between interesting events, with those events constituting our stories or our histories. However, it is in the everyday that we meet most people; that we prepare and eat meals; that we raise our children and that we engage in work and other activities. In short, it is in the everyday that we live most of our lives. The accounts given in this volume add to the Flashbacks project which will continue with further volumes by different people – perhaps even you.

This book has been jointly published by National Museums Scotland and the European Ethnological Research Centre. It reflects the National Museums Scotland's commitments to carrying out original research and to making the results widely available – commitments that underpin also the exhibition 'Land Girls and Lumber Jills' which opened in the National War Museum Scotland in February 2010.

Jane Carmichael
National Museums Scotland
EDINBURGH 2010

Mark A. Mulhern
European Ethnological Research Centre
EDINBURGH 2010

Auchincruive House, from the Thomas Annan Collection.
(*Source:* Reproduced by permission of The Mitchell Library)

Recruiting poster for the Women's Land Army produced as
part of the 'Lend a hand on the land' campaign.
National Archives, INF 13/140 (19).
(*Source:* National Archives of Scotland)

SCOTLAND'S LAND GIRLS

$\ominus$

Introduction

A Call to Scotswomen: Every woman who joins the regular force
in the Women's Land Army will take a soldier's place in wartime.[1]

AS the appeal went out for recruits to the Women's Land
Army (WLA) in newspapers, on posters, on cinema screens
and through organisations like the Scottish Women's Rural
Institute, so young women from a variety of backgrounds
answered. From schoolgirls working for their entrance to university, to young women working in shops and factories, they
responded to the nation's need. The WLA drew female labour
largely from urban Britain, and gave women the opportunity to
experience a way of living which was completely unfamiliar to
many of them.

Able to join at the age of seventeen years (though the point
was stretched for younger applicants on occasion), many of these
girls grew up during their years serving in the Land Army. Many
remained in the Land Army for the duration of the War – indeed,
when signing on, these women agreed to do just that, and a few
stayed on after the War as it was not disbanded until 1950.

The Women's Land Army, which included the Women's
Timber Corps, was originally formed in 1917. By then, the
increasing number of German U-boat attacks on ships bringing
food to Britain, and the relentless demand of the armed forces
for more men, had taken its toll on the nation's ability to feed

itself. According to some sources, Britain had only three weeks supply of food left, and the Minister of Agriculture referred to Britain as a 'beleaguered city'.[2]

The WLA was re-formed in the summer of 1939 when it became apparent that a second major conflict was inevitable. Early in World War II, U-boat attacks were more and more successful and the issue of food supply became acute, so the WLA was quickly expanded. At its height, over 80,000 women were members – 8,500 of them in Scotland. When the threat from U-boats lessened in the summer of 1943, WLA recruiting fell to a low level because women who might have joined were encouraged either to join the armed forces, or to go into munitions work or the aircraft industry.[3] Ina Lithgow recalled in her initial interview in Edinburgh, when asked which service she wished to join, she responded 'the Land Army' and was told, 'Well, we're getting kinda filled up now ... but I'll see what we can do'. Unbeknown to Ina, she was one of the few who managed to get into the Land Army in 1943. This was the year in which the number of women in the Land Army reached its peak.

The WLA's activity in Scotland was concentrated in the Lowlands, mostly in Ayrshire, Lanarkshire, Fife, Renfrewshire and Dumbarton, the Lothians, Dumfriesshire, Roxburghshire, Stirlingshire, Clackmannanshire, Angus and Berwickshire. Dairy farms, in particular, needed women for the never-ceasing work of milking cattle. In contrast, arable farms, such as those in East Lothian, demanded concentrations of labour at certain times of year, especially during harvest. The most appropriate way to meet this fluctuating demand was to house Land Girls in hostels and send them out to farms as and when required. This was reminiscent of the long-standing pattern of using migrant workers, often Irish, to meet labour requirements. Individual farms in remoter locations were frequently looking to replace family members conscripted into the armed services, and employing a Land Girl was often an ideal solution to this problem. Girls were also employed in East Lothian in labour-intensive horti-culture. The number of Land Girls employed in counties such as Caithness, Sutherland and Nairn was much lower.[4]

Although the Women's Land Army and the Women's Timber Corps both had military-sounding names, they did not form part of the British Army. However, Lady Denman, Director of the Women's Land Army in England, did see them as a fighting force in some sense:

> The Land Army fights in the fields. It in is the fields of Britain that the most critical battle of War may well be won.

The stories of the girls in this book bring the work and daily experience of the Land Girls to life for us, the readers, so many years on. Their efforts resulted in the increased production of crops and the raising of livestock, and enabled the people to be fed during periods of food scarcity. With their help, between 1939 and 1945, an extra 500,000 acres had been brought into active food production. The girls' labour was vital, and so too was their commitment to the war effort on the home front.

Life in the Women's Land Army

A variety of factors influenced an individual's decision to join the Women's Land Army. These included, amongst others, the desire to stay on the land for those already familiar with it; the love of the outdoors and of animals; the wish to avoid going into munitions work, especially if this meant moving from Scotland to England; the desire to get away from home; the attraction of the uniform; and the enticing posters. Many and varied are the reasons given by the Girls, but none mentioned any sort of conscientious objection to serving in the armed forces.

When a woman had decided that the Land Army was for her, her first task was to complete an application form for the Department of Agriculture for Scotland, St Andrew's House,

Edinburgh. At interview she was asked about the type of work she was currently doing; whether she was 'inexperienced in agriculture'; whether, if accepted, she would prefer to be posted locally or anywhere in Scotland; and if she had any special qualifications, such as the 'ability to drive a motor car or handle horses'. The interviewer also considered whether:

> ... references as to the character of the applicant should be sought. Does she appear to be physically fit to undertake work on the farm when called upon to do so? Is training considered necessary? If so, do you recommend it should be (a) at an Agricultural college farm? (b) on a private farm with a view to subsequent employment thereon?[5]

Details of the applicant's physical measurements were also included in the written report. Following a successful interview, the applicant awaited a letter instructing when and where to go for their training.

Depending on the applicant's previous experience, or, perhaps more tellingly, the impression created on the day of the interview, Girls were sent either to an agricultural college such as Auchincruive, Ayrshire or Craibstone, Aberdeenshire, or directly to a farm to receive on-the-job training. Women who went to an agricultural college received a number of weeks training (which seems to have varied during the War), each week focusing on a different topic such as dairying, poultry, market gardening and field work.

Training was required to enable the Girls to work with mechanised farm machinery – anything from powered sheep clippers to the latest milking machines – as well as basic mechanical skills to get a broken-down tractor working again. Nevertheless, the Girls could not simply be taught to use agricultural machinery – they had also to be able to clip sheep using hand shears, or milk by hand, in case they were sent to a farm without such machinery, or to be able to carry on if the equipment failed.

For those from a rural background, being sent for training could cause some resentment. Betty Lowe was taken aback when told, despite having been brought up on a farm, that she was to take a three-week training period (see page 81). But for those from an urban background, formal training was invaluable and for many it heralded the beginning of a whole new way of life, which for some was to lead to a permanent change. If Betty, born on the land, was frustrated at being sent for training, then Ina Lithgow, born and bred in the industrial port of Leith, was equally disconcerted when told she was to report directly to a farm in East Lothian. Ina need not have worried though, because she was about to have the time of her life.

Uniforms were issued either by post or should have been waiting for the Girls at the training centre or billets, although this was not always the case. Anna Searson remembers arriving at Auchincruive where her uniform was 'issued, well it was a free for all really!'; and Ina Lithgow recalls all the Girls trying on various pieces of uniform and having a great time getting each others' sizes mixed up. It proved to be a real ice-breaker. As a temporary measure new Girls were sometimes asked to provide their own clothes until uniforms could be supplied (see Isabella Rankin's interview, page 119).

The standard uniform issued to each new recruit included fawn corduroy or gabardine knee-length breeches; an Aertex short-sleeved shirt; a green and red striped tie with the letters WLA in yellow in a repeating pattern; a green wool, v-neck jumper; socks and shoes; wellington boots, if they were available; a hat; a green felt armband with 'WLA' embroidered in red, with a crown above it; a Land Army badge; and camel-coloured dungarees. None of the Girls whose experiences are recalled in this book mentioned being issued with oilskins or sou'westers, although Betty Lowe does recall some colleagues who were fortunate enough to have them.

The uniform changed a little over time. In 1942 a fawn officer-style greatcoat was introduced, designed by Worth the couturier.

In 1949 the brown, schoolgirl-style hats were replaced by green berets, as worn by the Lumber Jills. Adapting the hats was one way in which the Girls could attempt to reflect a little of their own identity. After completing each six-month period of service, a Land Girl received a red felt badge, usually sent through the post, although occasionally issued to the Girl in person. Triangular in shape, each half year badge was made into a diamond when the full year's service was completed. They were sewn onto the armband.

All of the uniform was 'on coupons', which meant acquiring it was restricted by wartime rationing. Clothing coupons had to be used to receive the various pieces of uniform. When the rationing of clothing was introduced in 1941, each adult was allowed sixty coupons per year, later reduced to forty-eight. However, due to the nature of their work, the Girls were awarded an additional ten coupons per year.[6] In spite of this, one of Mona McLeod's strongest recollections was being cold. She commented, 'For any Girl working out of doors in all weathers, the uniform was grossly inadequate'.

Uniforms returned by Land Girls who had left the service were sent to a central or local depot to be sorted and if suitable, following cleaning and repair, were reissued. Sometimes pieces of clothing became redundant because at the beginning of their farming work many girls quickly became stronger and bigger, some of them needing larger clothes after six weeks in the country.

There appears to have been no attempt to match skills or natural ability towards particular types of agricultural work. Although the Girls were asked where they preferred to work, there was no consultation about whether they were sent to an individual farm as a solitary Land Girl or into hostel accommodation with a number of other Girls. Individuals reacted in different ways: Una Stewart was pleased to be the only Land Girl on her farm, whereas Ina Lithgow relished the company of the other Girls in her hostel. Conditions varied enormously, from stately homes and purpose-built hostels to accommodation that was similar to a nineteenth-century bothy, without a bath or another Land Girl for miles for company.

Pay and conditions in the Land Army were, in theory at least, the same throughout the United Kingdom. Any differences in wages were not as a result of location, but rather that, after the initial training period, the farmer paid the girls directly and thus variations were not monitored. Ellanora Sherry had first hand experience of this (see page 75).

At the outbreak of war a male agricultural worker was earning on average 38 shillings a week. This was less than half the wage of unskilled labour in other occupations, although farm workers did have subsidised housing and some foodstuffs were supplied. The Land Girls were paid 28 shillings a week and Lady Denman had to fight to secure even this rate.[7] During the period of the War, the WLA rates of pay rose and the Girls could earn extra money for taking on duties such as driving a lorry. It was at the farmer's discretion to reward good work, and this did sometimes happen:

> … a large dairy farmer, was so well pleased with his girls that he decided to pay them 4s. a week above their minimum wage.[8]

The Girls worked, on average, forty-eight hours per week in winter and fifty in summer. The additional hours of labour required at harvest and haymaking time qualified as overtime.

When Girls were sent to their first posting, the cost of travelling was met through the issue of travel warrants. After a period of six months, any Girl whose home was at least twenty miles from the farm she was working on could claim travel allowances. This, however, did not mean that because a Girl had completed a six-month period she would necessarily be granted holidays. These had to be negotiated with the farmer, perhaps with the help of the local representative. Paid holidays had not been the norm in pre-war years and understandably farmers did not want to offer this benefit to Land Girls. However, in 1943 Lady Denman won the right for all agricultural workers to have one week's holiday-pay per year. Unpaid holidays could be negotiated at local level.[9]

Although there was no formal sick-pay for Land Girls, there were mechanisms in place for those in need of assistance. For example, application could be made to the Royal Scottish Agricultural Benevolent Institute in Edinburgh.[10] If a Land Girl was seriously injured, she could apply for compensation. One unfortunate Girl, Jemina, a raw recruit, was working on a farm in Fife when she was involved in a nasty accident:

> Yesterday 8th March [1944] while employed at the dressing of potatoes at Easter Upper Urquhart Farm, [Jemima's] hair became entangled in the mechanism of the elevator of the potato dressing machine and her scalp was lifted off. She was immediately removed to Perth Infirmary and is in a serious condition but believed to be progressing at the moment as well as can be expected.[11]

Only in her early twenties, Jemima was to spend several weeks in hospital and several months recuperating. Eventually, after a thorough investigation into the accident she received a significant sum of money in compensation, some of which was used to buy wigs.

If the Girls needed advice, they could approach their Area Representative, and if living in a shared billet they could talk to the hostel housekeepers. Alternatively, they could refer to *Land Girl: A Manual for Volunteers in the Women's Land Army* which retailed at one shilling.

The Land Army was especially keen to make sure the Girls were not used as domestic servants in and around the farmhouse, although they were expected to clean their bedrooms. Nevertheless, Land Girls were on occasion asked – or told – to do domestic work. To refuse could prove difficult. However, the

Land Army had been created to improve the nation's food supply, not to clean farmhouses, and if a Girl was doing domestic work she could have her labour withdrawn by her Area Representative.

Efforts to support the Girls and make them feel like a cohesive unit were made both at local level and centrally. They had their own magazine called *Land Girl*. Produced in England, it had a dedicated section for the women in Scotland. It contained stories, a letters page, quizzes and advice on practical farming related matters. Although apparently available nationwide, none of the Girls interviewed for this book made mention of it, and when asked had no recollection of it.

The Girls were also encouraged to take part in local agricultural competitions – ploughing or hoeing, for example – and occasionally the Area Reps organised get-togethers, especially valuable for women who were the only Land Girls on their farm. Mona McLeod remembers the first time she set eyes on another Land Girl when her Area Rep. organised a tea-party for the Girls in Galloway. Many of these Area Reps. who are remembered with great affection by the Girls themselves, were known as 'Aunties'.

The Identity of the Women's Land Army

The Women's Land Army had a clear identity of its own which created a sense of unity. The WLA in England and Wales and the Scottish WLA[12] had much in common; daily tasks carried out by the Land Girls themselves, south and north of the Border, were the same, as were the conditions of enrolment, training, welfare, the uniform and the lack of hierarchical ranking. The uniform, in particular, gave a sense of unity. The greatest differences between the situation in England and Scotland can be seen in two areas: the administrative structure and the billeting pattern of the Girls.

In England the WLA had a Director, Lady Gertrude Denman,

and a headquarters, Balcombe Place, her stately home set in 3,000 acres. With democratic enthusiasm, Lady Denman ordered the rose beds to be turned over to vegetables and the tennis courts to become the site for housing livestock. His home now filled with young Land Girls, Lord Denman retreated to Scotland and sent venison occasionally to supplement their rations.[13] In Scotland the WLA was administered from Edinburgh by the Department of Agriculture for Scotland.

Acting for the Secretary of State for Scotland, the Department of Agriculture managed farming through Agricultural Executive Committees. There was a Committee for each county, and they were largely made up of farmers and estate factors, plus a woman who represented the Scottish Women's Land Army. In addition, there was a chief SWLA liaison officer and three area assistants. Their particular role was to liaise between the Department of Agriculture and the Land Army sub-committees.[14] Although the need for agricultural labour was clear, simply applying for a post did not of course guarantee entry to a Land Army job. The 'right type' of girl was being sought. SWLA representatives were involved in the recruitment of suitable young women and their subsequent welfare. An application form from 1941 survives in the National Archives of Scotland and under 'General Remarks' it states of one candidate 'Superior working-class girl'; we can assume this particular girl was accepted into the Land Army.[15]

Due to the nature of Scotland's farming, the billeting pattern of the Girls differed somewhat from that in England. Although many Land Girls were housed together either in purpose-built hostels or houses that had been turned over to this use for the duration of the War, the Girls were much more likely to be sent out as lone Land Girls to individual farms than their colleagues south of the Border. Betty Lowe tells of her feelings on her first night at the farm at Auchrannie, Perthshire which she thought '… must have been the last place on the face of God's earth' (see page 89).

Despite its clear identity and important role, the WLA and

individual Land Girls were sometimes subject to strong and unhelpful prejudices. Some farmers, particularly in Scotland, believed that Land Girls could not work effectively. The writer and socialite Vita Sackville-West notes in her book published in 1944:

> Scottish farmers, I regret to say, took less kindly than their English colleagues to the idea of employing women. ... With the increased demand for labour and thanks to the good work of which the Girls were proving themselves capable, the prejudice gradually wore down. ...[16]

However, it is easy to think that initial prejudices held by some men against women were due simply to sexism, although it is certainly true that there were farmers who preferred to employ male prisoners of war rather than women. Nonetheless female labour, usually that of family members – so often hidden from official records – had been used on farms for centuries, so perhaps farmers' reluctance to take on Land Girls was based more on a dislike of 'toonies' coming onto the farm.

Such attitudes were deliberately countered by poster campaigns and testimonials which appeared in newspapers and magazines. This is one of several examples that appeared in the *Farming News and North British Agriculturist*:

> 'Land girls are better than men at certain types of farm work,' Mr George Morton of Laigh Newton Farm, Darvel, told the Secretary of State. He added he would advise farmers to take the Women's Land Army seriously, if the members were all as capable as Miss C. McRiner of Edinburgh, who was employed by his son. They would be a very valuable asset indeed.[17]

As well as having to tackle the prejudices of the farmers themselves, Land Girls sometimes had to deal with the insecurities and hostilities of the farmer's wives. On occasion this could result in a Girl requesting a change of farm. For the most part, the experiences of the Girls featured in this book do not fall into this category, and many felt warmly welcomed into the family with life-long friendships being made.

Fortunately attitudes did change and prejudice was overcome relatively early on in the War. This was largely due to positive experiences of farmers combined with their increasing workload as the Ministry of Agriculture required more land to be put under the plough, and the inability to find male farm workers. Additionally, as directed labour for women had been introduced in 1942, it became more acceptable for women to move into areas of work previously seen as male.[18]

In part this inconsistent approach to Land Girls may have been explained by the position they held in society. They were not quite recognised as one of the services, yet many of its members would have been directed into this war service by Government, and of course they were playing a crucially important role in the survival of the country. It was a similar situation in which the Bevin Boys found themselves.[19]

After the Land Army

As each Land Girl's term of service ended, she received a certificate of thanks from the Queen and was permitted to retain some items of uniform. Official notification stated:

> Please return to the Department's store ... all items of your uniform equipment, irrespective of condition, with the exception of 1 shirt, 1 pair of shoes and either your greatcoat or your raincoat, which you may retain free of charge. You may also retain your Land Army Badge.[20]

At the time, the gesture to keep one or two items of the uniform was seen as less than generous by the Girls themselves, the WLA management, and in particular by Lady Denman, who had fought long and hard for improvement in the Girls' working and living conditions and for formal recognition of them. After the War, surplus uniforms, including those of the WLA, were sent to Continental Europe to support various relief operations. However, a great proportion of these surplus uniforms never made it there; instead they remained in warehouses for many years.[21]

In 1944 the Government stated that Land Girls would not qualify for assistance in any post-war education or training scheme.[22] Lady Denman was so disappointed by this that on 16 February 1945 she resigned. Land Girls worked consistently long hours at low rates of pay, and received no official recognition at the end of the War. However, in small ways their contribution was valued. After the War, any members or former members of the SWLA/WLA were welcomed at the Ex-Service Women's Club, 12 Drumsheugh Gardens, Edinburgh. In August 1946 a letter was written, describing the club which had been reopened in July of that year by HRH Princess Elizabeth as being:

> ... charmingly redecorated. It gives meals at moderate prices and there are 12 beds. Ex-members of the WLA and the WTC are eligible for membership.[23]

In recent years there has been growing awareness of the role of women in history generally, and in particular of their role during both World Wars. Exhibitions have been created such as 'The Devil's Porridge', which tells the story of the women who worked at the munitions factory at Gretna during World War I. Temporary exhibitions on the Women's Land Army have been held at the Weald and Downland Museum in Sussex, Brighton Museum, St Barbe Museum in Lymington, Hampshire, and the National War Museum, Edinburgh, amongst others. Monuments too have appeared, which highlight women's contributions. Women of the Timber Corps were recognised by the

Forestry Commission in October 2007 when a bronze statue was unveiled near Aberfoyle; and in 1995 a memorial garden to the WLA was opened in Norfolk, the same year the twenty-two foot high National Monument to the Women of World War II bronze statue was unveiled in London, marking their contribution to the war effort. It shows the range of work undertaken by women by representing their uniforms or working clothing. Books such as Tyrer's *They Fought in the Fields* and Powell and Westacott's *The Women's Land Army* started to appear in the 1990s. In addition, a number of books were written by the Girls themselves. More recently, a wonderfully illustrated book by Gill Clarke was published to accompany the exhibition 'Land Girls: a portrait' (2008).

There have been other forms of public recognition. On 19 August 1995, Land Girls marched through London to mark the fiftieth anniversary of VJ Day. In 2000, former members of the Women's Land Army were for the first time invited to lay a wreath at the Cenotaph on 11 November. Finally, in December 2007, the United Kingdom Government responded to growing calls for formal recognition of the contribution that these women had made, by announcing that they would be awarded a medal the following year. Thousands of former members of the Women's Land Army applied for the badge, the design of which encompasses both the Land Army emblem – the wheat sheaf – and the spruce tree of the Timber Corps. The Girls assembled at ceremonies all over Britain, attended by Royalty, Members of Parliament and Lords Lieutenant to mark the occasion. Much pleasure has been derived in having their work recognised, and in once again having the opportunity to gather together to share memories of a time which, for many, was to change their lives.

WRITTEN RECOLLECTIONS

Jean Forbes Paterson

Early Beginnings

THE early beginnings of my love affair with the land and nature started with the genes passed down from my father whose family had been farmers for generations, and my mother who loved the house and garden to be full of flowers of all colours and perfumes.

By the time I was born, the eldest of three children, my father had retired through ill health, but had stock grazing in fields, hills and moors he rented in the district. A much respected figure in farming circles, he has been described to me on many occasions as 'one of nature's gentlemen'. He died two weeks before my fourteenth birthday after years of illness, so I never knew him as a person in his own right.

From the time I could walk, he took me with him in a great heavy tub of a car, an open tourer, as he did his rounds inspecting his animals. I think I remember this – but perhaps it's only hearsay.

Berry Time – or Going to the Berries

We lived in a raspberry-growing area. Uncle Jim, an uncle by marriage, had fields and fields of raspberry bushes at the Beeches. They were grown in straight lines or drills. Wooden posts, an even number of yards apart, supported wires at three different heights, to which the bushes were tied for support.

'Berry Time', as it was called, started about the second week in July. The farm, situated on the perimeter of the town, employed a squad of local people as berry-pickers, who returned year in, year out.

As a young child I loved to go with my Father, who was the 'Gaffer', and help him supervise and sort out minor problems. As the years passed, David and Beth, my brother and sister, came too.

Bob Tait reigned supreme over the 'gantry' [weighing station] and money box. It was he who weighed the pailfuls of berries and paid out the hard earned cash. On average, a picker was paid at the rate of a halfpenny per pound of berries (in old money). Not a handsome sum.

Jimmy Duffy looked after Chance the horse, and carted trailer loads of laden barrels to the station. To us he was just 'Duffy' and we loved him. He told us amazing stories about his fictitious 'Granny' (an old Mother Riley character) who supposedly travelled the country on an ordinary child's scooter with a tent slung over her shoulders. Her favourite holiday destination was Blackpool. She had fantastically exciting holidays and the most extraordinary adventures befell her. All these stories were told while he filled empty hundredweight barrels full of water to swell the wood, so preventing leakage of juice when filled with rasps. When Duffy himself had a holiday we always received a postcard signed 'Duffy's Granny'. We were very proud of this collection, which was nailed to the wall of the pail shed. We played tricks on him which would be blatantly obvious, but he always played along with us and acted accordingly. When we had grown too old to believe all the stories, we still asked after the health and whereabouts of his Granny.

My burning ambition over the years was to become a berry-picker and make my fortune. Berry bushes had been planted across the corner of a field; the first drill just a post length, but each row became longer. Selected berries for table and jam orders were picked there. That is where I began my berry-picking career, at the age of nine to ten years, and indeed my initiation to the farming world as a worker.

The squad started at half past seven [in the morning], so after they dispersed I was supplied with a 'luggie' – a straight sided small pail which was tied round my waist – and a large pail. My father escorted me to the corner, took my pail to the next post, threw a handful of berries into my luggie and left me to get on with it. Every now and then he would return to ensure I was finding and picking all the ripe fruit hidden below the leaves, say a few encouraging words, throw some more handfuls of berries into my luggie, and be off. I didn't suffer from loneliness, I was too busy dreaming of the fortune I was making and what I was aiming to buy. Each post length, I emptied my luggie into the big pail before transporting it to the next. This went on till the big pail plus the luggie were heaped with berries, then came the excitement of the weigh-in at the gantry. How much money had I made? I always set myself a target, higher each day at the height of the season. At the last weigh-in of the day, if Uncle Jim was about he would occasionally ask how much I needed to attain my target; if necessary, Bob would get the nod and my aim was achieved!

I would go home each evening, tired, scratched from the bushes, footsore and hungry, with clothes and hands purple with the dye from the raspberries, fair-haired, a lock at the front bleached nearly white. After dinner came banking time. My maternal grandfather, the only grandparent I ever knew, had made me a beautiful wooden bank in the form of a book, with the title 'How to Save by Jean Paterson' inlaid on the side. Each night the money was counted and recounted [and then] totalled – and the dreams went on. I went to bed, closed my eyes, and saw raspberries the size of plums hanging in great clusters. The next [thing] I knew, it was morning.

Over the years David and Beth joined me. David picked like mad for the first pailful, then off he would go to buy five wood-bine from a corner shop he frequented. Beth, the youngest, disliked the work, could not stand toiling in the heat, and would become tired and go off to visit our Aunt.

This particular year my heart was set on a bike, so I worked harder than ever. When I had made £1 (quite a sum of money in those days), I asked Uncle Jim if it would be enough to buy a bike. 'Of course it will,' said he. 'I bought a bike, plus a load of glass in an assorted lot at a farm roup [auction] a month ago for a pound.' You can imagine what my father went through. We trailed round every bicycle shop in the town to no avail. It was wartime, no new bicycles were being manufactured, and second-hand bikes were scarcer than gold. Eventually Father obtained a Raleigh from a friend whose daughter had outgrown it. It was the greatest thing I ever owned. In my imagination it was a horse, a car, a plane, a tank, and I toured the countryside on it. Never met Duffy's Granny though.

One dry sunny morning on my way to the berries, I fell off my bike on a very rough road. I skinned my knees and elbows, but worse than that I broke the thermos flask and burned my hands with the boiling water. I was more concerned about admitting to breaking the flask than about my injuries, as flasks were nigh impossible to find.

The time came when I was thought old enough to join the squad. That summer my general knowledge of life widened and deepened considerably. The squad had a few real characters in it who were perhaps inhibited by my enlistment, but [they] were back to normal within a very short time. I just kept my head down. I heard all the local gossip and the repartee was magic to listen to. However, there was the sadness of war. The son of one of the characters was killed. He was an RAF pilot. That was a quiet summer. We were all bereaved. Meanwhile the work went on. Some of the berries went to jam factories, but I think most went to make dyes, depending on the contract for a given season.

A few years later, officially a Land Girl, I helped Isla weigh the raspberries at Maryfield. They were poured into TUNS, huge barrels to which the chemical [sulphur dioxide] had been added for preservation purposes. It took the colour out of the berries and they became a very, very pale pink. The fumes from the chemical could take one's breath away, so it had to be handled very carefully. However, there is an upside to everything. Occasionally these tuns came with the residue of the last commodity – sherry – whisky – once alcohol of 100% [proof], which we siphoned out before refilling with pale pink rasps.

Some of the raspberry farms were huge and relied on squads arriving from Dundee and Glasgow every year. Whole families lived side by side in long huts in very primitive conditions. They worked hard all day, then enjoyed parties and ceilidhs; for some it would be the nearest thing to a holiday they would know. A berry-picker was the very first drunk I ever saw. He was lying in the street ranting and raving as my mother and I passed by. I was afraid and the incident left a marked impression on me.

These days there are houses built on some of Uncle Jim's land, and on the rest is the High School and playing fields.

I to the Hills

As I grew into my teenage years, life was very difficult at home as my Father was ill. I had to take on responsibilities, some of which were beyond my capabilities, but in time I grew into them. Being the eldest, I supported my Mother in every way I could, but in between I played hockey for the school, organising my chores to suit. However, everyday schooling and my chores started to suffer.

Part of each school holiday I spent time at the hill farm of friends twenty miles up the glen; Aberdeen Angus cattle and Blackface sheep were bred and reared there. Looking back, I must have been a real pain in the neck. Every morning I was ready awaiting the day's work, bright but quietly full of enthusiasm – it was a great life. For Bob the farmer and Willie the shepherd, there was no escape from me.

I helped to treat the sick and the lame. At lambing time I

would [often] hurry back to the farm kitchen with a sickly new-born lamb inside my jacket to help keep it alive and warm.

There were hundreds and hundreds of black faces bobbing and swimming in a shimmering rippling sea of wool, when the whole flock was gathered together for docking of the lambs' tails, worm drenching, clipping and dipping. For events like these, farmers and their shepherds would help one another by moving round until all the sheep in the area had been treated. Many times I was swung over the dipper too. The noisiest gathering by far was when the ewes and their lambs were separated. The poor things bleated pathetically as lambs searched for their mothers. I found it difficult to sleep that night, but by the next day peace had returned.

There are many memories in my head of those years. I used to go and blether to Willie in his bothy and he played good-going tunes on his melodeon. A tower silo stood high above the steading. I climbed it first thing in the morning and last thing at night during the summer. I was a bit scared of heights, so I had mixed feelings about the ritual, and I don't know why I made myself do it. It was the first place where I ever drove a tractor and I nearly rammed it into a large oil drum in the back of the tractor shed! A dynamo machine stood in the steading. It was used to generate electricity, otherwise it was paraffin lamps in the house and tilley-lamps, which had special mantles, for outdoor use in the steading.

There was one painful occurrence. I was in charge of a horse and a cart with a load of hay or oats being taken to the steading. I had been instructed to be very careful when I came to the narrow gateway in the dyke. I was so absorbed in this manoeuvre that somehow the horse managed to bring its shod hoof down on my heel. It was agonizing. My heel was blistered and became very swollen. For days I had to wear Bob's wellington boots, the only footwear large enough to encompass the bandage.

Winter was the time to work with the young Aberdeen Angus bulls in readiness for the February bull sales in Perth. They were given the best of food, they were groomed – highlighting all their best qualities – they were clipped; they were pampered; they were walked up and down in halters. I was given instruction on how to judge – what to look for, both good and bad, in an animal. I walked them up and down so that John the cattleman could observe them as if in the ring. My Father died the week of the bull sales, so I couldn't attend that year. The war in Europe ended on the 8th of May and I spent most of my summer holiday on the farm, working with the sheep, and especially the lambs being groomed and made ready for the lamb sales.

That was the year I was introduced to electric fencing and strip grazing.[24] Rape had been sown in the spring and the very best lambs, the ones for showing, were fed on short stretches of the field each day. I was scared to go near THE WIRE. Bob, knowing this, would grab the wire and my arm simultaneously, and I would jump about a foot in the air from the shock. I learned not to walk within yards of him if he was near such a fence. A few years later we used strip grazing in dairy farming. It saved good grass being trampled and allowed the cropped section to grow again very quickly.

The lambs were dipped and groomed, their horns filed and oiled, their feet kept in immaculate condition. The excitement and tension rose. But I had to go back to school! On the day our lambs were due to go in the ring, I took a day off and went to the sales. In the market, Willie and I were giving the lambs a few last minute touches of perfection when someone asked to photograph us. We agreed, thinking nothing of the incident.

I had a great day! The reckoning had to follow! My mother refused to write a letter explaining my absence. I walked to school next morning milling over in my mind different stories to put forward. In the end I arrived, hoping against hope nobody had missed me. My form mistress played cat and mouse with me for a short time, because emblazoned on the front page of her daily newspaper was my photograph with the caption 'Intent on Work' above it. That same teacher some months later, in front of the whole class, gave me the severest dressing down I had ever had. It was over a maths paper which merited me with ten out of a hundred marks! She knew me well; at the next maths exam I came second in the class. Years later we met and became good friends, with a mutual respect for each other.

Unfortunately, school and I continued to drift further apart. At weekends and later, after school, I would make my way to the farm up the hill from where I lived. The farm was about to change from mixed farming to dairy farming and work started on reconstruction of some of the buildings.

After many heated discussions at home with my poor mother, I was allowed to leave school, on the promise that I would attend agricultural college at a later date.

On the 19th of July 1946, I officially became a Land Girl.

Dairy Milk

4.30am. A summer morning, the sun shining, the air fresh, birds singing and soaring – the world seemed brand new and I was the only person on earth.

Collecting the dogs, we padded together towards the field in which the small herd of Ayrshire cows was crowding together at the gate, their full udders being their time clocks. On other mornings it could be a very different picture, with torrential rain pouring down like a hail of bullets coming from all directions when blown by a strong wind. In these conditions the cows would be standing with their heads down, facing the stone dyke, refusing to move, no matter how I yelled and waved my stick, or the dogs barked and snapped at their heels.

In summer the long lush grass becomes laden with water, so even when protected by wellington boots and a long mackintosh, my knees would be soaked and the rain always managed to run down my neck, saturating my shirt collar.

During the cold dark winter months, the herd was kept in reeds [cattle-yards or bays] within the steading. So, every morning the milking cows were standing waiting for us to start the milking. They were warm and alive, some of them even kicking! Their coats, hairier and longer in winter, gave off a warmth that was sleep-inducing as we leaned against them during milking. To combat this, we played a black wind-up gramophone which blared out the music of the era. 'NOW IS THE HOUR'!

Over the years the herd grew until we had over sixty milk cows. Each was given a name and we could recognise every cow individually. Like people, they were all different; some were small and dumpy, some were large with big bone structure, some thin, some fat, some gawky, some self-possessed. Their markings varied too; some were dark with white areas, some were ginger coloured, while Sheila, if I remember correctly, was pure white all over with large dark eyes and long eyelashes. Margo, on the other hand, was dark brown with white rings round her eyes.

They all had different personalities; some timid and tranquil, some brutes and bullies, others were highly strung with staring eyes, ready to kick out at the slightest provocation – those we became expert at side-stepping. Others were more wily, with tails that would twitch and lash across an unsuspecting, unprotected face in an unguarded moment during milking.

The milking parlour had spaces for four cows to be milked simultaneously. The machines would be attached to the cows and a steady *choo! choo! choo!* pulsed round the parlour as the milk was sucked up and squirted into glass jars.

After each cow was milked it was released back into the reed and replaced by another cow. Meanwhile, a master tap emptied the jar and drew the milk along a gleaming pipe, which carried it through the wall, where it rippled over the milk cooler in the adjoining room. Under the cooler sat the bottle filler; it had a sliding platform on which the milk crates were placed. By pulling a handle on the side, five bottles were filled at a time and a heavy hand clamp sealed the silvery foil tops. The crates were then stacked in readiness for the milk round.

Some of the remaining milk was used for feeding calves and

the rest was collected by the Milk Marketing Board[25] in large ten-gallon churns.

Washing up

A predominant memory of that time was the amount of water that was sloshed around. The floors and walls were hosed down before milking and scrubbed down afterwards. Cold water was sucked up and drawn through the whole milking system, followed by hot soapy water, then a cold rinse, [followed] by steam under pressure which hissed along, ensuring absolutely everything was sterilised.

There was a washing-up room next to the engine room and through the wall from the cooler room. It contained two very large galvanised tubs. Above the tubs sat the bottle washer. This was a small electric engine which propelled three brushes: two for the insides of the bottles and the third larger brush for cleaning the outsides. After the bottles were washed, they were rinsed in cold water contained in the second tub, before being placed upside down in their crates, ready for sterilising.

The cooler, the bottle filler and other sundries were washed at the end of the milking, and sterilised while we were delivering the milk. The steriliser sat in a hole in the wall between the washing-up room and the cooler room. It had two doors, one in each room, so it was filled up on one side, and the sterilised contents removed in the clean cooler room.

The cacophony of sound during this process was deafening. There was the clang and clatter of the crates, the rattle of bottles as they were tossed into the galvanised tubs which responded with bangs and booms, the splutter of the bottle-washer engine and the whirr of the brushes; there was the gentle clink of the bottles bobbing against one another as they floated in the rinsing water, and the clank and clang of the milk churns which were scrubbed inside and out before being sterilised on a jet of steam specially designed for this purpose.

The steam that rose off the water, which was often too hot to handle, did great things to my soft baby-like hair, and the freezing cold of the rinsing water in the dead of winter caused the hacks and raw hands that pained me till the coming of spring. There were [also] scalded hands as the extremely hot bottles coming out of the steriliser had to be turned right end up.

That was work! Then there were the water fights during the more clement weather, while we were sweeping and washing down the walls, floors and dairy steps. Pails of water were emptied energetically in all directions, not always aimed at what we were cleaning! On at least one occasion I was thrown into the tub of cold rinsing water, where I was held down till my clothes were saturated. I dripped all the way home in water-filled wellies.

A day came when the bottle-washing machine petered out. A new part was needed. This meant the bottle-washing was post-poned until evening. Around seven we faced over one hundred and fifty dirty milk bottles. Isla, my partner in crime, produced a bottle of sherry she had won in a raffle, and I was introduced to the dark depths of the Devil Drink.

The sherry – heavy, dark, sweet and possibly very cheap – we drank from the best crystal half-pint milk bottles on the market. To begin with, the work went with a swing and a song, but as we were packing the steriliser, I was the one who was starting to swing and sway. I was advised to retire for the even-ing, so I adjourned to the cottage where I played and sang along with the black wind-up gramophone. By the time Isla came in, I was looking in a very puzzled way at the gramophone as the turntable would not revolve. You know why? I was leaning on it with my elbow. Very shortly after that I had to rush to the bathroom, where I vowed I would never ever drink alcohol again in all my life. In fact, for years and years I couldn't look at a bottle of sherry without shuddering.

So you see, even when doing the most mundane jobs, we managed to sing, laugh and enjoy life with all its ups and downs.

Cow Power – Horse Power

The 'Milk Round', taken over from a 'dry' dairy in the town, started from a very humble beginning – sixty-four pint cartons to be exact.

During and immediately after the War, no commercial or private vehicles were manufactured. Spare parts for existing vehicles were nigh impossible to find – so it was make do and patch up again and again. Petrol was also rationed and coupons had to be produced before fuel was allowed to flow into a petrol tank.

At first we used a 1938 ten-horsepower Vauxhall car. The milk cartons fitted snugly into specially designed wooden boxes, two of which filled the boot, while the rest nestled into the back of the car once the rear cushion was removed.

Over a period of time, all this extra weight became too much for the gearbox, which would jam in third gear sometimes more than once on the way round. A screwdriver was carried at all times! The gear lever had to be removed and the gearbox manoeuvred into neutral, allowing us to continue our deliveries.

On another occasion the accelerator cable snapped. *Ooh, help!* Hanging on tightly with one hand, I perched precariously on the wing, controlling the speed of the car by pulling on the cable attached to the engine. Imagine the joy and excitement of a sixteen-year-old with all that power at her fingertips. We waltzed, tangoed and kangaroo-hopped all the way home.

I loved that old car because I taught myself to drive in it when I was fifteen and a half to sixteen years old. I never had a driving lesson of any kind. First of all just round the farm; then, growing bolder, down to the town where I parked at the Episcopal Church. From there I walked for the shopping which, as often as possible, included a chocolate cake from Keiller's the bakers. These sorties added a wee bit of fear and spice to my day.

Once, reversing too fast for my capabilities, the back near-side wheel mounted the dairy steps. The car rocked a few times, as did my nervous system, but fortunately kept its balance. Mysteriously, a few weeks later the rear spring gave up the ghost. I still blush at the thought!

We delivered milk in all conditions, seven days a week, all the year round – on clear fresh mornings, in pouring rain, in howling winds and in ice and snow. We shot round as fast as the prevailing weather allowed, sprinting on a warm summer morning or lumbering along in wellies and heavy Land Army mackintoshes in more harsh conditions.

We had running battles with fierce growling dogs. Many and varied strategies were used to outwit them as they came at us like shots out of a gun. The two worst offenders that I can recall were a black labrador and a liver-and-white spaniel, two soft-mouthed sporting dogs that are usually quiet loving animals.

There were children who thought they were helping, and old ladies who couldn't find their purses anywhere on pay-day. There were also those who hoarded their empty bottles for days or weeks and returned them all sticky, smelly and unrinsed.

One severe winter for about six weeks, we had to deliver the milk by tractor and cart after opening the farm road which, each morning, was filled by drifting snow. Apart from the crates of milk, we had to carry shovels and sand. This was to give grip to the wheels, especially where the children had been sledging the previous evening, polishing the snow to a hard glittering surface under the new soft snow of the night.

It was cold! Everything was wet or frozen. Our fingers stuck to the frost on the metal crates and the sides of the tractor, and at times snow blew in our faces and lay in layers on our eyebrows and eyelashes.

By the time the thaw came we were worn out shovelling, gritting, moving crates, sliding, slipping and slithering up and down garden paths. We had blisters and hacks on our hands and chilblains on our feet, which itched and burned as we sat at the fire in the evenings trying to dry clothes for the next day's trek.

Over the years the demand for locally produced milk grew

steadily, and three vans, stacked with crates, left in different directions each morning, distributing hundreds of pints to the doorsteps in the community. Girls often sat on the back swinging their legs, hanging on to crates of milk, ready to slip off as the van slowed down.

Milk Recording

Dietary patterns are forever changing. Today, with the medical world checking cholesterol levels, weights and blood pressures, dairy products are forbidden foods for many.

In those days, just after the end of the War, customers expected to find two inches of rich cream filling the tops of their milk bottles and many had standing orders for cream. We sold both single and double cream every weekend for Sunday lunches and for special orders during the week.

Milk recorders were employed by the Milk Marketing Board. Each had a district to cover, visiting the dairy farms to calculate the quality and quantity of milk each farm produced. Every cow was tested for her butterfat level and the quantity of milk yielded during her lactation. In this way a poor producer, or one with a low butterfat level, could be culled from the herd.

Jimmie, our milk recorder, a real character, brightened our lives once a month. He would arrive in his van amid a cacophony and a clatter made by all the paraphernalia of his trade, a big battered suitcase and his piano accordion. He stayed overnight in the farmhouse, but once fed he would arrive on the cottage doorstep with his piano accordion over his shoulder.

A tall, broad, blue-eyed guy with blond wavy hair, he knew all the topical jokes and had many tales to tell picked up on his rounds. He played the accordion and we all sang and probably shared a beer. They were good evenings.

Early mornings were a different matter. We had to start the milking earlier than usual because Jimmie took samples of milk and documented the quantity yielded from every cow. The samples, in small glass tubes, were clipped into a centrifuge machine which spun at great speed, separating the butterfat from the whey.

Space was limited in the wash-up room cluttered with the miscellaneous instruments he used, as we washed up after milking. On top of the usual clamour there was also the constant whirr of the centrifuge machine. Breakfast was a lifesaver. Then we were off on the milk round, so Jimmie was left in peace to his calculations and documentation. Usually by the time we returned he was off to his next farm.

Once in a while inspectors from the Milk Marketing Board would suddenly appear and take samples of milk from the ten-gallon churns and milk bottles. These were tested for bacteria – also for water percentage!

The Vet

Anyone having an animal or animals knows the value of a good vet and how expensive treatment can be. We had a good one, worth his weight in gold. He also had an old MG open sports car that I fancied.

He paid us a yearly visit when the whole herd was tuberculin tested. That meant that every cow and calf was rounded up on two occasions: the first to be given the test and again to check the result.

As the cows were wintered in reeds and occasionally tempers got a bit frayed, great damage could have been done with sharp pointed horns. Hence all cows had to be dehorned. That meant giving them a slight whiff of chloroform and the deed was done using a small saw. My job was to place wads of cotton wool over the horn stumps. There was next to no blood and certainly no casualties. The calves, when young, had their horn buds treated with caustic stick which prevented growth, so no horns grew.

The bull was a different story. He lived in a loose box and one day took a great dislike to Henry the German POW who looked after him. He tossed Henry right across the loose box where he managed to climb up on the hay-rack and yell for help. It was decided that the bull's horns would have to be amputated. The whole farm team grouped together and a complicated strategy was planned. He was given a tranquiliser and brought out into the reed on a pole attached to the ring in his nose. Hobbles and ropes were fixed in place and everyone was instructed when and in which direction to pull. We managed to take the feet from him and had to stay in that position, keeping the ropes taut until the operation was over. The vet gave him a massive dose of chloroform to knock him out. The vapours of the anaesthetic rose up and nearly overcame the vet, whose face became whiter and whiter as he sawed through those massive horns. Afterwards the bull slowly got to his feet, the shackles were removed, and on shaky legs he was led docilely back to his loose box. Believe me, we were all mightily relieved.

The vet helped with the difficult calvings. He would turn a calf that was being born the wrong way round. He gave drenches to ailing cows and instructed us how to do the same. On occasion he would examine a calf that was not thriving, or stitch a lacerated teat, or a cut in a dog's paw.

Once, he did a post mortem. In the early days of hay-balers, wire was used in the machine to tie the bundles of hay together. A cow had ingested a piece of wire along with a mouthful of hay. She suddenly dropped dead and the vet was sent for. Being a ruminant, she had a stomach divided into four compartments which the wire travelled through. The wire had a pointed end and a hooked end; the hooked end had caught in the stomach wall, but the pointed end had pierced her heart. It was a very sad occasion, doubly so as she was carrying a calf which was too young to survive.

Another hair-raising experience happened when the young clover was too rich and probably wet. A cow eating too much of this rich grass blew up like a drum. If the farmer hadn't had the presence of mind to stab her in the side with his pocket knife, she would have died too.

Vets are called out in all weathers and at all times of the day or night, but ours was always pleasant and kind to whichever animal he was treating.

Spring-time

Spring! The threshold of a new year in the farming calendar. Life took on a new meaning. A spring was in our step too, as outside work gained momentum. The ploughs made great furrows as the dark, damp earth was turned over, or a green field ploughed for the rotation of crops. Be it on your own head if those furrows were not straight! Then came the discing and harrowing, until the great clods of earth were broken down into fine textured soil in readiness for seeds to be sown. Drills were formed for the planting of potatoes and the sowing of turnip seeds. The fields allocated to be the hayfields of the year were rolled to firm up the earth and help thicken the grass. When rolled properly the fields resembled a croquet lawn.

The soil was fed with fertilizers or with manure taken from the 'midden' or the reeds. In the days before dung spreading machines, this had to be done manually, a deeply odorous occupation. We walked miles planting potatoes, backwards and forwards, up and down the drills – a foot-weary, back-breaking job. I trotted behind a turnip seed machine too, for acres and acres. Oats, wheat and barley were sown also by a much bigger seed machine, from large bags of seeds deposited at the end-rigs which had to be heaved and hauled for re-filling purposes. Occasionally peewit's eggs would be found, lying open to the world, in a drill. Nowadays it is rare to see a peewit, which is a great pity. Where there was new ground to be cultivated, large stones had to be lifted onto a cart and driven to a dump – another back-breaking job.

It was a noisy time with tractors purring and growling in adjacent fields, pulling different implements clanging and rattling behind them. Gulls wheeled and called as they followed the plough.

The weather over this period of time could vary from snow showers, sleet, rain, freezing cold winds and April showers, through to a softer, subtler promise of the summer to come. As the earth dried, strong winds blew dust in our eyes making them water, so we ended up with mud-encrusted eyes, noses and lips – a terrible sight to behold. We were often soaked to the skin or stung by hailstones; other days we were stiff with cold. However, as time marched on the weather would improve gradually, so by the time the turnips needed thinning out, if we were lucky, we acquired a wonderful tan. Over these weeks the whole country-side flourished. The grass grew thicker and greener and the trees became decked all over with leaves and blossom. The sun rose higher in the sky and the days lengthened.

About this time 'pit-silos' became fashionable. The first cut-ting of grass from the hayfields was packed into a pit along with strong smelling sweet dark molasses, and stamped down by running a tractor back and forth over the top. This was repeated, load after load, until the pit was full. The whole area was covered by a deep layer of earth and a tarpaulin, which was weighted down by old tractor tyres and left to ferment till winter.

All through the busy buzz of this spring work, the everyday work was carried out as usual. The cows were milked, calves were born and fed, milk delivered, bottles were washed and sterilised. Hens were fed and eggs collected. Implements for use during the haymaking were hauled out of dark corners where they had wintered, and were patched up ready for use.

By the end of May the cows were turned out into the pasture for the summer. This set into motion the cleaning of the steading inside and out. Walls were scrubbed and coated with Snowcem [a white cement-based paint], doors were painted green and the runners they moved on were always black.

In the fields the drills were refurred to keep the potatoes and turnips well covered with soil as they grew larger.

As our day started at half-four with the milking, these were very long, very fatiguing days. And most of the field work that we did was carried out in the evening till dusk drove us home.

Oh, for that much energy today! I wonder, was it partly due to the quantity of Keiller's chocolate cake consumed?

Hay-time

In the early days of the milk round, with only sixty-four cartons of milk to fill and deliver, and no bottles to wash and sterilise, we were home and in the fields in the forenoon. However, that changed over the years as the retail milk sales escalated. The herd also grew, so milking started earlier both morning and afternoon, and took longer to complete. There were more calves to feed too. Therefore our time spent on general farm work became limited to a few hours in the afternoon and in the evening; hay-time and harvest were exceptions.

Grass grew tall, sweet and succulent, ripe for cutting. The hay-cutter was taken from the dark cavern of the implement shed into the light of a June day. The teeth of the cutting arm were sharpened until they shone like silver. The wheels and all moving parts were oiled.

Dave, the farm grieve, and one of his men, armed with scythes, would cut swaths of the rich grass, opening up a road all round the field in readiness for the tractor and mowing machine, officially beginning hay-time.

There was the purr of the tractor and the fumes of combusted paraffin, and the swish and click of the teeth on the cutting arm as they slid back and forth felling the high green stalks of grass. There was the clank and clunk of the metal wheels hitting a stone or uneven ground, and the scent of the newly-cut grass lying in straight swaths, hopefully drying under a hot sun. If the weather was kind, the grass dried and became sweet smelling, light and airy hay. It was turned manually with pitchforks in those days before the coming of hay-turners and balers. During a wet season it was turned and turned again, between bouts of rain, while the hay was becoming darker, less sweet and eventually moulding. Successful farming depends so much on the weather.

The hay was then lifted off the moist ground and built into 'coles' around wooden tripods. This allowed the breeze to blow under and through, keeping the hay fresh and well ventilated. From the coles the hay was transported to the stackyard adjacent to the steading, where it was built into huge stacks by the grieve and his team. This meant all hands on deck.

Two tractors and trailers were used. The trailers had 'haiks' fitted back and front. These were wooden slats which rose high and wide, so huge loads could be built and kept in place. While one cart was being loaded in the field, the other was being emptied in the stackyard. Sometimes we had extra help from casual workers and then from German POWs from a nearby camp, who helped with the forking. Being the youngest and shortest, I usually had the job of building the load on the cart. A long, long time has passed since then, but if I remember correctly the basics of building a cart was to build round the outside of the cart, keeping the corners wide then filling in the centre, all the while trampling the hay, packing it down, trying to make this will-o'-the-wisp mass into something more solid under my feet. Every inch had to be filled, or as the load grew higher my leg would suddenly disappear down a narrow tunnel.

In the heat of a summer day, it was exhausting on the arms and legs as I tried to distribute evenly the fork-loads being heaved at me, sometimes from different directions. The aptitude of the forkers played a big part in helping or hindering me. An expert would lay his fork load exactly where I wanted it. Others didn't even know to turn the fork, so that the prongs were not facing me as I received the hay. This was dangerous on a jolting cart! Remember, some of these men were Germans with language problems and knowing nothing of Scottish country life. Thistles were another constant peril – green growing thistles are jaggy – but once dried they are lethal. They stuck and broke under the skin of fingers and any bare skin with which they came in contact. Cartload after cartload was built as I became thirstier, hotter and hungrier. I would start to pray for the 'midser' break, milking time or nightfall as my legs and arms started to tremble with fatigue. ... I had [a fear] of jumping off the top of the high load and hitting the ground, with the possibility of some of the load coming with me.

There was a great deal of pride associated with the building of a cart. The load had to stay in place as it was joggled and jangled by the tractor juddering along a very uneven road to the farmyard. [You could be] the butt of much derision if the worst happened!

The haystacks were built in the yard, then thatched with wheat straw to keep them dry and sweet until used for winter feeding. Then they were tied down with ropes weighted by stones. Only then was hay-time over.

There was the risk of hay heating in the stack if it was wet when harvested, causing ignition by combustion.

Autumn – Harvest-time

As the seasonal clock moves round to autumn, the sunshine becomes softer, kinder, more golden. The days grow shorter, the nights chillier. Then comes the time for harvesting cereals, potatoes and, later, turnips.

The grain harvest followed much the same pattern as hay-making. Broad roads were cut round the fields and sheaves were tied by hand to allow the binder or harvesting machine space to manoeuvre into position. The binder had a cutting arm (as the hay-cutter had), plus canvas sheets, and wooden flails or paddles and a box with binder twine. As the machine moved forwards, the paddles turned, pushing a measured quantity of cereal on to the cutting arm. The cut lengths were then conveyed over the moving canvas sheets, where they were bound together into sheaves, tied with the twine and tossed out of the other side of the binder. High above the machinery bounced an observation seat on which some poor soul jolted, swayed and swung as the binder paddled its way through the stalks of grain.

The sheaves were then lifted by hand and made into 'stooks' to dry, hopefully in the sunshine. A stook consisted of eight pairs of sheaves leaning against one another – a back-breaking job. During a wet summer, whole fields of grain could be flattened, making the cutting tedious and time-consuming, as someone had to walk in front of the tractor trying to untangle the twisted stalks. The taking in of the harvest again saw me building carts in the same fashion as before, but instead of will-o'-the wisp hay it was fork-loads of sheaves, a much heavier, more solid substance. If, however, the corners were kept wide, it built into a beautiful tidy high block of gold shining in the sun. The thistles jagged as usual and very painful scratches were endured from the cut ends of the straw, especially strong wheat straw; but the anguish suffered from 'bear awns', the beards of barley, were intolerable. As the barley was being handled, these beards broke off and flew everywhere, sticking inside shoes, boots, stockings, shirts, down necks, in hair. Every movement was torture as they jagged and scratched. Ages were spent each night extracting them from clothing and skin.

The straw stacks were built in the stackyard, thatched and weighed down to be left until a threshing day during the winter.

Meanwhile, as the nights grew colder and longer, the milk cows were bedded down in the reeds overnight, so at 5 am there was no further need to look for cows in the dark fields.

The Potato Harvest – Tattie Howkin'

During the War, a percentage of the acreage of each farm had to be planted with potatoes to help feed the population. Schools closed for two weeks in October so that the children could help in harvesting the potato crop.

They were employed in 'squads' uplifted each morning by tractors and trailers, vans, open lorries with covered frames offering some protection if there was a distance to the field being harvested.

Each child was allocated a stretch of ground called a 'bit' (the younger children half a bit), marked off by whin sticks. He or she was responsible for lifting into wire baskets all the potatoes thrown out by the demon digger as it devoured drill after drill. No sooner were backs straightened, than the stooping and bending began again. How we all prayed for 'piece time', or dinner time. It was a tiring, back-breaking task, especially for children unused to manual work, or indeed the countryside.

The baskets of potatoes were emptied into carts which conveyed them to the 'pit' at the end of the field. The pit was shaped like the roof of a cottage, with a broad base sloping upwards to a narrow ridge for drainage purposes. The potatoes were lagged in wheat straw and a thick layer of earth to prevent water, snow and frost penetration.

To some it was an adventure, to others heart-breaking drudgery – the early rise in the morning, being rattled along on a trailer or lorry, sometimes in semi-darkness, wearing an odd assortment of old clothes (remember there was clothes rationing too!). Every piece of clothing cost a number of coupons and though there was a war going on, children still kept growing. There was the cold, the dark, the fights, the squabbles, the dirt, the mud, mud-fights, aching backs and broken fingernails. However, there are good memories too! There was the fun and games at the dinner break, and the potatoes baked in an open fire with solid bluey-black skins too hot to hold (but how good they tasted!). Turnips, stolen from a nearby field and eaten raw, filled an empty space quite nicely, tastier because they were plundered. We tried to feed baby mice whose nest had been blown asunder by the demon digger, and there were dreams of spending our 'tattie money' at the end of the holiday!

I was one of the children in a squad, then graduated to the emptying of the baskets and conveying the potatoes to the pit. An adventure or drudgery – it was a job that had to be done.

The Turnip Harvest

The most poignant memory of 'shawing' turnips was the excruciating pain caused to the hands. Each neep had to be lifted manually from the earth, tailed and topped by a sickle, then thrown into the cart, with a constant bending and bobbing trying to keep up with the other workers.

The turnip harvest followed on behind the tattie lifting. The weather deteriorated, the days grew shorter and darker. Trees were naked to the elements. The earth held more and more moisture with permanent puddles forming. Alternatively, frost sparkled like stardust in intricate lacy patterns on dykes, and hedgerows and ice covered puddles and turnips froze solid.

There must have been many days that were dry and pleasant, but it is the high and low memories that remain in the mind. Even piece times were less enjoyable than breaks in spring and summer. First of all, we each had to make up our own 'piece', which had to be eaten standing up or precariously perched on tractor or trailer. Our hands were filthy and wet with cuts sustained from misdirected chops from the sickle. As always the repartee would ricochet around, but it would slowly die down as the day progressed and darkness came down.

Having splodged along all day in muck, boots or wellies had to be scraped and hosed down before going home. Hands had to be treated with TLC [tender loving care!] and brought back to life. When very cold, an icy gap developed between the skin and clothing, and it took a long soak in a hot bath and a good meal to bring back a relaxed warmth to the body.

Some of the turnips were lagged in a pit like the potato crop, while some were stored in the turnip shed for immediate use as feeding. At one time Isla and I used the turnip cutter daily, a hand-operated implement (which worked on the same principle as the domestic egg-slicer) to slice turnips for animal fare.

There was also an old-fashioned washing boiler in which we boiled potatoes to mix with bruised corn to feed the free-range hens. And of course, busy with other chores, we would forget to restore it. A quaff of paraffin would be thrown on the rebuilt fire, an explosion would echo round the turnip shed, and once more the spuds would be on the boil!

The turnip crop was the last to be harvested. Winter settled in and a new routine commenced.

Winter-time

There was a gradual build-up to winter, when a completely new regime came into being. All the instruments and machines used throughout the year, from sowing to harvesting, were cleaned and oiled before being stored in the implement shed. They were placed in the correct order, with the binder in the back and the ploughs, discs, harrows, drilling machine and seed barrows in front, for the next spring.

As the nights grew longer and colder and the first frosts gripped the land, the milk cows were brought into the reeds overnight for shelter. During the colder weather their coats grew longer and thicker, so electric clippers were used to shave their hindquarters and udders for easier cleansing at milking times. They were groomed weekly during their stay inside and fresh wheat straw was spread in the reeds each morning after their departure. In the evenings, turnips and hay were fed to the cows to help them settle down for the night. [Cattle] cake was served in the milking parlour which helped to keep them calm during milking, the amount depending on the yield of each cow at a given time.

In the dark, cold mornings it was more difficult to crawl out of bed, but there was one consolation – no rounding up of a reluctant herd in a dark field. With the switching on of the steading lights, the cows would start to rise and stretch, then patiently wait to be admitted to the parlour and a session of music from the black wind-up gramophone. Then one dark cold morning they would be kept in for the winter. The young heifers and dry cows (cows in calf) would be housed for the winter too.

All round the outside of the reeds were feeding troughs, enough for the number of cows housed there. Animals, like people, have different personalities and temperaments. Some were bullies, while at the other end of the scale were very nervous timid beasts – often newly-calved heifers were in this category. To ensure each animal received its ration, heavy hinged trellises were mounted in position, so when every cow found a place – sometimes with help – this trellis was locked in position, making certain that all were fed in a peaceful fashion.

They were fed twice daily with a snack at lunchtime. Hay was forked from the hay-shed and, later, bales were cut and forked when hay-balers came into vogue. The pit silo was opened and the strong pungent smell of silage prevailed in every corner of the steading. It clung to clothing, skin and hair. Special dungarees were worn inside wellies and kept only for feeding times. The first winter Isla and I managed all this between us, but, as the herd grew and the milk round developed, Dave the grieve started to help with the feeding until Henry the German POW arrived to live on the farm and took over those tasks.

I thought Henry was a mean man. I was very wary of him. He roared and shouted in a coarse way. Once, after cutting the string on a hay-bale, I laid down my pocket knife while I forked the hay into the hayracks. He picked it up and shouted, 'Who finds keeps, who loses greets!' Furious at such an underhand trick, I watched him like a hawk for weeks until he did the same as I had done. Without a word, I pocketed the knife, which always stayed there when not in use, from then on.

Winters nowadays seem to be dark with RAIN! RAIN! RAIN! In those days there seemed to be more snow and ice, with no double-glazing or central heating in farm cottages. My bed was heaped with blankets and, after sleeping like the dead, I would crawl out in the mornings, stiff as a board flattened by the weight. Ice formed on the inside of window panes. The outlet pipe from the bath would freeze, and in pre-Rayburn days we had an old black range that had to be coaxed and chivvied into life each morning – if we had time.

A silent muffled stillness would indicate a deep snowfall, and looking out very early in the morning an eerie white light would be penetrating the darkness. If the snow was accompanied by gale-force winds, huge drifts would be whipped up into immense mountains of magnificent peaks and patterns. The farm road would be blocked, morning after morning. Subsequently it had to be cleared manually to allow the passage of the Milk Marketing Board lorry and the vehicles used for the retail deliveries.

When frost followed the snow, millions of diamonds sparkled and reflected all over the fields in a dazzling display as in a child's fairy-tale. However, rain caused inches of wet slush which penetrated all but wellington boots, which are not the warmest of footwear. Sometimes slush was frozen into hard ridges, making walking and driving tortuous.

Passing through the steading at the end of a very long hard tiring day, an immense feeling of peace and tranquillity would wash over me at the sight and sound of very satisfied cattle, lying chewing their cud and exuding a fine vapour into the air.

There was a warmth and a simplicity about the scene that remains with me to this day.

The Threshing Mill

My maternal grandfather trained and worked as an engineer with the LMS [London Midland & Scottish] railway line until a horrible accident resulted in the loss of his left thumb. Being left-handed, it meant the end of his career with the railways.

A friend who lived nearby owned a traction engine and a threshing mill. He employed my grandfather to drive and maintain both of these machines and soon they became business partners. The traction engine pulled the mill from farm to farm around Montrose and the County of Angus. It also powered the mill while threshing the grain. Threshing day was a 'red letter day' on every farm, when all the stacks in the stackyard would be forked and fed into the mill. Farmers and farm workers would gather from surrounding farmsteads to help each other. The women folk would congregate to cook mounds of food for the hungry masses at midday and at the midser times.

Many decades later, I remember as a very young child the excitement when a shiny, well-oiled black and green traction engine rumbled majestically up the hill past our home, like a ship in full sail, pulling a great wooden contraption on the way to the farm, where I would later attend threshing days.

As the hay, straw and grain stored in the barns and granary were almost exhausted, the time came for opening the stacks in the stackyard. [It was] a relatively simple task – removing the waterproof thatching covering the tops of the stacks, forking the hay on to carts and transporting it to the steading, and packing the hay-shed.

The cereals had to be milled! Most farmers at that time had to book the travelling mill going round the circuit. We were lucky! There was a threshing mill built into the steading, so we could thresh as much or as little as was necessary at any time. As I write this, I realise it was a unique feature for a farm to have one in those days. However, by the 1960s, combine harvesters had taken over.

Threshing day meant noise, fumes, choking dust and more choking dust. It was a much noisier exercise than the outside mill because of being in such a confined space. While the stack or stacks were being opened, the old orange tractor which always sat in the corner of the tractor shed was filled with fuel and had to be cranked and cranked to be started. It had a power drive which, when attached to the mill by heavy thick leather and wire belts, suddenly put life and vigour into the monster machine. The tractor had an upright exhaust, so all the fumes rose and floated in great grey clouds just under the low roof of the tractor shed. The fumes of the combusted paraffin also added to the delights of the day.

The mill having been inspected, repaired and oiled where necessary, large hessian sacks were attached underneath in readiness to catch the golden grain which would slide down the chute.

The tractors, loaded with sheaves from the stack, would draw up under a doorway set one storey up in the wall. Everyone had his or her designated post and specific job to do. When everyone was in place, the tractor power drive was put into gear and the noise was deafening.

The sheaves were forked in through the doorway, the strings on them were cut, then they were fed into the open mouth of the monster mill. The noise was indescribable from the tortured sheaves as they were torn apart. They screamed and screeched. There [was] the whine and rattle of the grain as it buzzed about in the belly of the machine, the crack and snap of the belts as they whipped the mill into a frenzy, the clanging of mechanised parts seen and unseen, and the roar of the powerful old tractor charging away in the tractor shed.

The straw came spewing out and constantly had to be forked into the straw-shed opposite the mill. Dust and chaff swirled and danced in the air like demented souls; it filled our eyes and our noses were lined with it as we inhaled each breath; it stuck to the sweat on our faces and arms and lay like a cobweb on our hair. The huge sacks of grain had to be lifted off the mill and manoeuvred to the foot of the granary stair. Voices were raised to try and communicate with each other, and a great deal of tick-tacking went on with not a racecourse in sight.

When the last sheaf had been processed and no more straw or grain exited from the mill, the power was shut off and the old tractor was left to sleep in the corner. A deathly silence took over and we all stopped shaking and vibrating. The grain was carried up the stairs to the granary and the area was swept and tidied. It was one of the few days during the winter months that we all worked together as a team. Threshing day was over once again.

Tractors and Vans

Just as [the dogs] Nick and Tweed were extensions of us while working with the herd, tractors were indispensable on the cultivation side of the farm.

Prior to agricultural mechanisation, a ploughman's day started around five. He was responsible for mucking out the stable, feeding, watering and grooming his charges, before harnessing them for the morning's work. At mid-day, having trudged up and down a field driving his pair of horses while controlling a plough, or harrows or a potato digger, depending on the season, he took them back to the stable where he watered and fed them before deigning to partake of his own 'piece'.

At the end of the working day, he would undergo the same scenario before relaxing for the evening. A ploughman and his horses became close companions. Most nights he would check that all was right before he himself retired. This regime extended over the weekend, except in summer when the horses were turned out to pasture. How they whinnied and galloped in pure delight at their freedom, like children freed from the classroom. The coming of the tractor put an end to this and the companionship was lost between man and horse.

The farm was fully mechanised and up-to-date for the era when I took up my duties. The start of the day for field workers was seven o'clock. The man who had toiled previously behind his horses sat upon his iron steed which could accelerate well beyond the speed of a working horse. Over the years, implements have grown larger and more sophisticated. Today a plough can turn over six furrows at a time instead of one.

There were three tractors, all very different characters indeed. They all started on petrol, then when warm ran on paraffin.

The Old Orange Tractor

Big, heavy, cumbersome, slow and noisy! She had metal wheels with projecting lugs as she trundled and trudged from one lug to the next, gouging out great ruts on the ground, not a smooth ride! This vehicle never required to be road taxed as it never left the farm.

She had to be cranked with a starting handle to bring her to life. She had a kick like a mule and could easily have broken a wrist of anyone attempting to start her. It was very difficult to engage a gear, even with the clutch pedal on the foot plate, and the noise and vibrations from the gear lever grated on the ears and the arm. She was used for very heavy jobs, and Isla usually had the dubious honour of ploughing with the old lady. Most of the time she sat in the corner of the tractor shed where she powered the indoor threshing mill. At the end of a day working with her, every bone and muscle ached and quaked long after the engine ceased to roar and silence was indeed golden!

She was called many names!

The Green Fordson

It was lighter and less noisy, but faster with good pulling power. The accelerator was a ring pull with notches on the arm, so it could be set to any speed in any gear. Like the old 'orange lady', it had big broad mudguards on which, if not driving, I could sit while moving to the next job of work. It had large solid rubber wheels with thick treads made for more comfortable travelling. The tractors all had metal seats, perhaps with a hessian bag or an old jacket folded on it to make life more comfortable. On the Fordson the seat was on the end of a metal arm, so one could bounce along quite nicely or drive standing upright for a change. This was the tractor Dave and I used for milk deliveries up and down the steep streets during severe winters.

The Ford Ferguson

It arrived with its silvery paintwork gleaming, not a scratch nor a scrape in sight. She was a racehorse in comparison to the Fordson [in the] Clydesdale mould. The driver sat atop like a jockey. Lighter in weight, she was much faster off her mark, quieter and good for town work. She had a hydraulic lift so that matching implements could be lifted and lowered with little effort by the user. She also had an independent braking system, useful on many occasions.

I enjoyed driving these machines. What teenager wouldn't? The one exception was reversing the cart into [the] cart shed at the end of the day! Limited space did not help the situation.

One other event that remains in my mind happened in late summer while working by myself. Pulling an old binder behind the Ford Ferguson, I was topping grass in a steep field. I took too sharp a turn on the hill and the weight of the binder made the front of the tractor rear up and its back wheels spin. I remember placing my jacket and hessian sack off the seat, under the back wheels before I managed to move off again. In my mind's eye I could see the binder, followed by the tractor, careering backwards down the hill and landing in a broken heap at the bottom.

These tractors saved much leg-work throughout the seasons; ploughing, sowing, planting, carting off stones from a new uncultivated field, carrying all the necessary equipment and tools for fencing and draining or mending dykes. At hay-time and harvest, through to helping in the milk delivery in the dead of winter, they were a great help.

Isla

Isla was tall and slim with dark brown eyes and brown hair with a hint of auburn through it. She had a warm smile and a ready laugh. I can see and hear her so clearly in my mind, throwing her head back as she laughed heartily. She always looked neat and tidy under all conditions, while I looked like a rag bag. Even-tempered, she never showed much anger and always saw the funny side of a situation. She had a real strength of mind and character which has remained with her throughout her life.

During the war years as a Land Girl, Isla had lived alone in the cottage in a calm, comfortable fashion. Then a sixteen-year-old was thrust upon her which must have shattered her peace and tranquillity. Imagine the shock to her system, but she never showed it. This was over half a century ago, and to this day we remain firm friends. Being a lot older than I, she became my family and mentor. She taught me much about work and guided me through the perplexities of growing up. We laughed a great deal and shared a special language that nobody else understood.

Neither of us was very domesticated and I was probably untidy, so we would have a massive clean up every so often. Isla did most of the cooking (probably for self-preservation), while I was supposed to set the table and do the washing-up.

The cottage consisted of two bedrooms, a living room, a small kitchen and a tiny bathroom. The living room housed a Rayburn stove which ate anthracite. If we were rushed at break-fast time and forgot to rake and re-stoke it, it would just die. Have you ever tried to ignite cold anthracite? I expect a little paraffin helped on a few occasions. When looked after, it kept the water hot and the living room warm, but the other rooms felt like the Arctic during the winter, and pipes froze. In summer the reverse happened – the heat was stifling and all windows were open as wide as possible. But no matter the climate, we always had hot water.

One very hot August evening, Isla had gone with a friend to a party being held in a shooting lodge. Beth, my sister, was visiting and using my room, while I was trying to sleep on a camp bed next to the Rayburn. A thunderstorm rolled around in the distance, slowly growing louder and louder and more menacing, like the approach of an angry fire-spitting dragon. The claps of thunder roared and crashed, while the flashes of lightening lit the whole night sky. Then the rain came! The heavens opened, pouring out an overwhelming deluge of water. I remember running round closing all the windows. I found Beth cowering in a corner, terrified to close the window for fear of being struck by lightning. Meanwhile the rain was spraying in, soaking the foot of her bed. Water was flowing like a river in spate down the mud track which passed as a road in front of the cottage garden. Overhead the thunder and lightning continued to chase each other with great glee.

Time came to gather the cows and start the milking. But where was Isla? The storm had quietened down, but there were burns and great lakes of water everywhere, deep puddles and new holes in the farm road, with stones washed to the surface. The cows of course were reluctant to move. Beth was instructed on what to do in the milking parlour. We would have to cover for the absence of Isla. Just as I came into the steading with the cows, Isla's car was seen coming up the hill. Thank goodness! Her friend had refused to travel by car during the storm, no matter how Isla had pleaded with her.

During the winter months we were glad to close the door on the dark and whatever weather was prevailing. We doctored our chilblains and, on my part, my raw hacked hands. During hay- and harvest-time we spent ages with a needle probing and removing thistles from fingers.

Wellington boots – very necessary footwear in the dairy and in wet fields – rubbed great holes the size of tatties in the heels of our socks or knee-high hose. Remember this was before the age of nylon and wool socks. Instead of darning, we knitted squares in thick wool and sewed them into place.

We read a great deal, nodding off between times. We listened to plays on the radio and were avid fans of Tommy Handley's 'ITMA' ['It's That Man Again'] and such like programmes. Having a catholic taste in music, we listened to anything from classical music to hit songs of the day. The Squadronaires playing dance music was a favourite on Saturdays at lunch time, while the wind-up gramophone could be heard blaring out the music of the 1930s era. Cole Porter music is still the tops with me to this day. Last week I found, to my delight, a Charlie Kunz CD playing the same melodies we had listened to over half a century ago.

We enjoyed a very limited social life. Occasionally we would attend a concert or a dance, but our early start in the morning was prohibiting. Therefore we were content with the quiet life.

Looking back, life with Isla was a mixture of hard work, fun, more hard work, joy and laughter and great contentment. I see her in so many different situations; driving the heavy, battered orange-coloured old tractor with the iron wheels, working the dogs, herding the cows, sitting on the back of the van, legs swinging ready to hop off at the next stop on the milk round. Forking sheaves, feeding the cows with hay, covered in dust and straw as she heaved great sacks of grain off the mill.

I can hear her singing as we tried to harmonise the latest hit song while washing the milk bottles, and I can still feel her presence walking beside me.

We are still in constant contact and I feel very privileged that she has been my life-long friend.

Dave

Dave the farm grieve, though not very tall, was broad shouldered, with dark eyes and wavy black hair, and a wide mouth showing strong well-spaced teeth often chewing on a piece of straw. He wore his bonnet at a jaunty angle and, while he talked, he would lift it, scratch his head and replace it in his own jaunty style. Sometimes he wore 'nicky tams' for protection while doing very dirty jobs. He lived with his wife and, at that time, two children in the cottage adjoining ours.

Ian the farmer and Dave would discuss the workload for the day, or in fact the week, and Dave would organise the team. By the time he became grieve, the dairy side of the farm was developing rapidly, so we – Isla and I – had less time to spend on field work, but we fitted in where possible. Before Henry the German POW came to stay on the farm, Dave helped us with the winter feeding of the cows.

During the very severe winter … he was the one who assisted me on the milk round: by helping to open the blocked farm road, driving the tractor and moving the milk crates around so that the full bottles were accessible to me at all times. Together we even sanded hilly parts of some streets, where children had sledged the evening before. We became quite a team.

In the spring I reciprocated by working in the fields during the evenings. That meant working until the job was finished or it was too dark to see beyond the tractor. That was in the days of double summertime, so it could be very late indeed. Dave was always waiting in the tractor shed for whoever was working late, as he refuelled the tractors in readiness for a quick start in the mornings.

As I was the youngest member of the team, he at times teased me unmercifully. I learned to take the flak, hold my counsel and retaliate when the opportunity showed itself. But he also had to rely on me delivering plough socks and such implements [that were] being repaired at the Smiddy; and also, on the quiet, pieces of machinery that had inadvertently become broken and needed welding.

I see him building stacks, covered in dust on a threshing day, expertly reversing carts into the cart shed at high speed, forking hay, barrowing turnips to the cows, clipping the cows as they come in for the winter often covered in snow.

Twice a week he visited the Dreadnought, a local pub, for a pint and a game of darts. This was a ritual. I think I dared join him on one occasion; in those days women were not seen in a pub – it would be a dare!

Dave eventually left to manage a large arable estate. Unfortunately, he received terrible injuries when a combine harvester

FIG. 1

Jean Forbes Paterson being taught to shear with hand-clippers, *c*1946, Perthshire.

(*Source:* Jean Forbes Paterson)

FIGS 2(a) and (b)

Women's Land Army membership card belonging to Jean Forbes Paterson.

(*Source:* Jean Forbes Paterson)

You are now a member of the Scottish Women's Land Army.

Your country welcomes your services.

You are pledged to hold yourself available for service on the land for the duration of the war.

You have promised to abide by the conditions of training and employment of the Scottish Women's Land Army; its good name is in your hands.

Your work on the land is of vital importance to the nation; by doing it well you will be performing a national service and helping to win the war.

Your country relies on you to do your best in the national effort.

Patrick R. Laird.

Secretary, Department of Agriculture for Scotland.

I realise the national importance of the work which I have undertaken and I will serve well and faithfully.

Signed *Jean Paterson.*

TO BE SIGNED BY VOLUNTEER.

The local Women's Land Army Sub-Committee has been entrusted with the duty of looking after the welfare of volunteers.

On being placed in employment, the volunteer should enter here the name and address of the local Women's Land Army representative, to whom she should refer for advice if in difficulty regarding her conditions of service, accommodation, etc.

Name *Mrs. Moon.*

Address *Balhomie.*

Meiklour.

Name

Address

Name

Address

Department of Agriculture for Scotland, St. Andrew's House, Edinburgh, I.

Wt. 944 4/42

SCOTLAND

MEMBERSHIP CARD

Name *Jean Paterson*

Home Address *Auchenclown,*

Newton St.

Blairgowrie.

W.L.A. No. *29387*

Date of Issue *19th July 1946*

W.L.A. I.

FIG. 3
Jean Forbes Paterson (far left)
with pals on a Fordson tractor,
*c*1946, Perthshire.

(*Source:* Jean Forbes Paterson)

FIG. 4 (*below*)
Wartime Identity Card
belonging to Jean Forbes
Paterson.

(*Source:* Jean Forbes Paterson)

FIG. 5 Ellanora Sherry (*née* McLaughlin) (far left),
on a day off from her Land Army work, *c*1943, Lanark.

(*Source:* Ellanora Sherry)

FIG. 6 (*above*)
Ellanora Sherry (*née* McLaughlin)
(front right), *c*1943, Lanark.

(*Source*: Ellanora Sherry)

FIG. 7 (*above, right*)
Elizabeth (Betty) Lowe
(*née* Wyllie), *c*1943,
Craigeassie, Angus.

(*Source*: Elizabeth Lowe)

FIG. 8 (*right*)
Una Stewart (*née* Marshall) using
an evacuated milking system,
*c*1943, Angus.

(*Source*: Una Stewart)

FIG. 9 (*right*)
Una Stewart (*née* Marshall)
helping a calf to feed from a
bucket, *c*1943, Angus.

(*Source*: Una Stewart)

FIG. 10 (*left*)

Marion Allison (*née* MacMillan) in the WLA uniform, *c*1942, at Westerhouse Farm, Carluke, Lanarkshire.

(*Source:* Marion Allison)

FIG. 11 (*left, below*)

Marion Allison (*née* MacMillan) was joined for a short time by another Land Girl, Elsie Graham (later Todd), *c*1943, Carluke, Lanarkshire.

(*Source:* Marion Allison)

FIG. 12 (*below*)

Laura Bauld (*née* Lindsay) using a Rotovator, *c*1948, East Lothian.

(*Source:* Laura Bauld)

FIG. 13 Laura Bauld (*née* Lindsay) with her future husband, Willie, at Greenend Farm, *c*1948, East Lothian.

(*Source:* Laura Bauld)

FIG. 14 Laura Bauld (*née* Lindsay) with an unnamed boy, hoeing, *c*1948, East Lothian.

(*Source:* Laura Bauld)

FIG. 15 (*left*)

Anna Searson (*née* Murray) on a trip to the photographer's studio, 21 August 1943, modelling the full WLA uniform, including the hat, Ayrshire.

(*Source:* Anna Searson)

FIG. 16 (*right*)

Studio portrait of Isabella (Isa) Rankin (*née* Barker) in her Land Army uniform, minus the hat! Taken *c*1942, while serving at Pencaitland, East Lothian.

(*Source:* Isabella Rankin)

FIG. 17 Isabella (Isa) Rankin (*née* Barker) (second left) with colleagues
at Dovecot Market Garden, Haddington, *c*1943.

(*Source:* Isabella Rankin)

FIG. 18 Mona McLeod (far right, behind the hedge) at a tea-party
organised by Mrs Jessie Grierson, SWLA Representative for Galloway, 1941.
Despite having served for nine months, this was the first opportunity
Mona had had to meet other Land Girls.

(*Source:* Mona McLeod)

FIG. 19 Mona McLeod (left) with fellow Land Girls, Bobby Stubley and Doris Brown, enjoying a little time off, *c*1941, Solway Firth, Galloway.

(*Source:* Mona McLeod)

FIG. 20

Mona McLeod in her WLA uniform and doing her favourite job as a Land Girl, working with the horses, *c*1942, Galloway.

(*Source:* Mona McLeod)

Fig. 22 (*below*) Margaret Watson (*née* Macbeth) (right) wearing WLA dungarees, taking a well-earned break with her sister, *c*1948, Lanarkshire.

(*Source:* Margaret Watson)

Fig. 21 (*above*)

Margaret Watson (*née* Macbeth) wearing an old battle-dress jacket, scything, *c*1948, Lanarkshire.

(*Source:* Margaret Watson)

Fig. 23 Petrina (Ina) Lithgow (*née* Seaton) standing (back, right) next to her former school friend Agnes Boyle (*née* Flucker), East Lothian, *c*1943. Ina and Agnes remain close friends to this day.

(*Source:* Petrina Lithgow)

he was working on slipped off the jack, pinning him across the chest. He never fully recovered.

I remember him as a great guy to work alongside.

Frank

Frank was a tractor driver – a tall, thin, quiet, nondescript man who travelled to and from work on a motor bike. He never had a great deal to say, but he must have had a sense of humour to put up with the rest of us. He patiently tried to teach me to reverse the carts into the cart shed each evening. It was a difficult manoeuvre, as it was impossible to have the tractor and trailer in a straight line to start with because of the lack of space. It took me ages! Derogatory remarks and much laughter from the audience accompanied my over-steering and shunting backwards and forwards, until in the end I conquered the exercise.

One morning Frank arrived on a brand new black and red motorcycle. Oh, the excitement! – he was so proud of it. No one was allowed to drive it but himself, though he took each one of us for a short spin on it. I remember sitting on the pillion seat back-to-back with Frank, bent low over the back wheel circling the steading – backward!

The other cameo picture I have of Frank was during a party we held in the cottage. Frank had a bit more to drink than usual and his rendering of 'A Slow Boat to China' was unforgettable.

He married and led a life we knew nothing about, for he lived outside the farm. The rest of us formed a small community, bound together by the confines of the farm, the seasons, and the weather.

A Boy called Dan

He was younger than I by two or three years; he was on the plump side and had flaming red hair. Disaster followed him everywhere he went, and hardly a day passed without some breakage or calamity befalling him, or so it seems in retrospect. He was always in hot water!

I remember him reversing a machine into a dyke, which had to be rebuilt, while the implement had to be taken for repair by the blacksmith. This held up work for at least a day.

Once when carting large stones from a field high up on the hill, he managed to end up with the tractor on one side of a fence with the cart still attached, entangled in the fencing wire. He had had so many 'tickings off' that for a while, if he landed in trouble he would come looking for me. I became the buffer between him and authority.

… In the end he left the scene of one crime and walked home, never to return.

German Prisoners of War

The German prisoners of war were held in a camp about eight to ten miles from the farm. An Army truck deposited them at the farm each morning and collected them around half-five. As time passed they were allowed to walk down to the town to be uplifted, very conspicuous in their light green battle-dress uniforms. They became familiar figures and some of the residents in the street started giving them sandwiches and cigarettes, exchanging a few words in stilted German and English.

A short, stocky, fastidious English major, with stitching down the edge of the creases in his trousers to keep them razor sharp, kept a record of their hours worked and their general behaviour.

Christoph and Henry became regulars and ultimately came to stay in the 'bothy', which we cleaned and painted for their benefit. It was furnished in a frugal way with beds, chairs, tables, cutlery and basic necessities before being passed as adequate by the major. Their main meals were cooked for them. Their coming put an end to the darts matches we had played and enjoyed in the bothy in the long winter nights. Our heating system was simple and explosive. Large logs soaked in a generous quantity of paraffin were pushed into the old black range. A lighted match was tossed in and after a mighty boom the logs burned merrily all evening.

Christoph was a quiet gentle contented man from one of the states over-run by the Nazis prior to World War II, and forced like a great body of his countrymen into the German military force. Looking back, I think he was glad to be a prisoner and enjoyed the limited freedom he had on the farm. He settled down into the life and was a good worker, very pleasant to work with and talk to. On two of my birthdays he brought me presents made of wood and painted either by himself or a fellow prisoner.

Henry, on the other hand, was a different matter – a big-boned man with a parting in his red hair just above his left ear and a red fringe edging out under his cap. He was both coarse looking and coarse mannered. While Christoph worked mainly with the outside workers, Henry fed and worked with the live-stock from late autumn to spring. There were many clashes of temperament and we had to watch him like a hawk. He was the one the bull tossed across the loose box. When the Army truck came to take him for repatriation, he stood at the tailgate as it started off downhill, shouting, 'Cheerio, you B_____s'! A few weeks later the same lad sent a letter asking us to forward him a tyre and inner tube for his bicycle!

Paul was a shadow of a man. Skin and bone, perhaps shell-shocked, he never walked if he could run and his movements were jerky and sudden. He always looked terrified and the level of communication with him was very low indeed. I often wondered what he was like before the War and how he survived on his return to his homeland. He was the first to be repatriated.

Adolph was a very skilled stonemason. He came to the farm daily and was kept in the work that he loved until he returned home. He built calf pens with sluice drainage for easy cleaning. They had metal rings attached to the wall to hold a feeding pail and each had a special drinking bowl and a small wooden gate for easy access. He planned and built a new double garage with a wash-bed in front which was used eventually to house the new Ford Pilot car with the V8 engine – the pride and joy of Ian the farmer – as well as the newest milk van. He repaired all sorts of buildings. He built walls, cemented steps, repaired dykes. He kept his head down, working steadily day after day, and every job was done to perfection. His English was a bit difficult to understand and he never put off time if there was a job to do, so I never had long conversations with him.

I wonder what their impressions were of the Scottish Farm Team?

Old Sandy

Sandy was a very old man, or so I thought at my tender age. His bald roof was surrounded by a thick thatch of hair and I can't quite remember whether he sported a genuine beard or whether it was very long stubble. Both hair and beard were white when washed!

He just seemed to drift into the farm community, probably having slept overnight in the barn as he was used to sleeping rough. I have no idea how much he knew about gardening, but he started to work somewhat intermittently in the farmhouse garden for pocket money.

This meant he was fed at regular intervals during the day. The next step was the lining of a vacant shed with plaster-board, which was then furnished with a black iron bedstead, an easy chair and a paraffin heater. He became ensconced in this little home like a king in his castle. He gathered together a few basic necessities and some days his face would be clean, his hair would be gleaming white, and all would be well with his world.

However, if he gathered too much cash together, he would go off to the town and come back full of booze in a quarrelsome, aggressive mood. Sometimes he would be missing for a few days, when he would arrive home much the worse for wear, with cuts and bruises from falling about and sleeping goodness knows where. On these occasions he was left strictly alone until the effects wore off.

Often I was sent to him with food on a tray and on many occasions I stayed and listened to many interesting yarns, which he would recall with a merry twinkle in his old blue eyes. He was always very polite and gentlemanly – he called me 'Miss Janey'; a good rapport built up between us and I became fond of the old devil. Looking back, I probably learned a great deal from our friendship.

Unfortunately, he fell ill and one day was whisked off in an ambulance; his way of life had caught up with him at last. In hospital he became so clean he was unrecognisable! From hospital he was taken to an old peoples' workhouse, where he died shortly afterwards.

Thinking back over the years, I can see him walking about, shoulders bowed, muttering to himself or sitting in his armchair chuckling to himself at stories I had heard over and over and over again. Remembering him brings back a very warm glow of gladness that our paths had crossed for a few moments in time.

[Now, a word about the farm dogs, Tweed and Nick]. Dogs are wonderful companions. They are loving, faithful, obedient – most of the time – and unfailingly good listeners who never talk back. They are great confidants who hear secrets and sorrows, and in return muzzle you lovingly with a cold wet nose to let you know they understand and are always ready for fun and games and food. Working dogs also know when it is play-time and when it is time for work. For a spell we had two dogs on the farm.

Tweed was a well bred, good-looking black-and-white long-haired collie, sweet tempered and obedient and very appealing to the eye; everyone loved him. He belonged to Ian the farmer, but we used him for herding purposes, very helpful especially on very wet days, when the cows were standing with their heads down, facing the dyke, refusing to move.

Nick, or Nicky, was not as handsome as Tweed … he was a smaller dog with a smooth, short black coat. When young he had suffered a bout of distemper, a viral disease very often fatal in dogs, and it left him with a constantly nodding head. Despite that, he was ever keen to work, sometimes being over enthusiastic. What he lacked in looks he made up for in character, and I loved him. One day Ian gave him away to friends taking up dairy farming. He was just bundled into the boot of a car and driven off. Months later he was used to herd some cows from his new home back to us and I went down to help them through the town. Nicky spotted me, and forsaking all else came charging straight at me, landing in my arms with his front paws round my neck. I don't remember ever seeing him again, but in memory both Tweed and Nick walk with me to this day.

* * *

Sixty years have flown by since the days I have previously written about. Farming has gone through many changes over the decades, with numerous ups and downs in the fortunes of farmers. Let us hope circumstances and conditions are improving once again.

Mechanisation having taken over many manual tasks and assignments, a farmer and his family may easily run a farm without the help of hired hands. Therefore farm cottages left empty have had their roofs removed to prevent paying council tax on each. Many have been rented or sold as holiday homes.

In the past ten years, between Foot and Mouth Disease and BSE, better known as Mad Cow Disease, plus diverse directives from Brussels, life has been impossibly hard for many farming communities. Perhaps with the lifting of the ban preventing British beef being sold throughout the world, farmers' fortunes are changing for the better.

The majority of surviving Land Girls will be octogenarians by now and their memories either faded dreams or nightmares!

The girls came from all walks of life; some straight from school or college, or business in town or city. A few had never visited the countryside, never seen a field, never touched a tree, or never knew the smell of earth following a shower of rain. On the other hand, they had never seen mud, nor smelled the scents of a farmyard nor been in contact with farm animals – so they were terrified.

They had never worn [wellies] or tackety boots! What a culture shock!

Away from home perhaps for the first time in very scary surroundings, having to rise early on dark wintry mornings, physical exhaustion, bumps and bruises, and most of all longing for home and family – yet in spite of all this, they fought on and won through.

This year on Remembrance Sunday [2005], the country commemorated the sixtieth anniversary of the end of the War. I was privileged to attend this service where I laid a poppy wreath on behalf of Alexandria Parish Church, and I was proud to wear my Land Army badge in my lapel.

During the two minute silence, I thought of all those known and unknown who never came back, and all those gallant girls who fought so diligently in the fields in all conditions.

I salute them one and all.

Ellanora Sherry (*née* McLaughlin)

I WAS still attending Elmwood Senior Secondary School in Bothwell at the outbreak of war in 1939. During the summer holidays in 1940 I got a job in the tax office in the Municipal Building in Hamilton. During the Clydebank Blitz we worked until nine every night, dishing out emergency ration cards to those who had survived but had no home left, and to soldiers home on leave but whose home or family had gone in the Blitz.

The air raid siren went every night and I hated it. There had been an outbreak of smallpox and we were all vaccinated, whether we had previously been done or not.

Across the road from the Municipal Building in Cadzow Street was the bank building, and in the grounds there were calves grazing. This appealed to me. I had an uncle who was a vet in Montrose and I fancied the life, and so I decided to join the Women's Land Army. Even so, it was my chum who posted the application as I hated the idea of a 'medical'. I need not have worried, as the doctor [only] asked if I had varicose veins – 'No' – then I was in.

I found myself training in the autumn at Auchincruive, West of Scotland Agricultural College, in Ayrshire. One week between pigs and poultry, a week on dairy, and two weeks in the fields bringing in the harvest.

Opening the pig sties at six [in the morning] none of us would forget, and yet pigs never soil their living area but always use a latrine which could be shut off from their pens and cleaned separately. This took a strong stomach and a sharing out of cigarettes. We did not have any breakfast until the animals were cared for.

The cows were sleeping in the field opposite the hostel where we lodged and at four o'clock we went into the field, roused them, and drove them to the byre for milking. The milking machines were much the same as today: four teat cups attached to the lid of large receptacles by means of rubber tubes through which the milk flows. These pails hold several gallons and are heavy to carry.

The cows knew their own stalls and sorted themselves out. We then chained them in, fixing a chain around the neck. In those days cows had horns. At Auchincruive we had Ayrshires – patchy brown and white, or black and white. After milking, the cows were released back into the fields and we set to with the mucking out. The animals were usually given a feed of cattle cake or turnip while being milked.

During the first fortnight of training, we came back for breakfast after seeing to the animals. The next two weeks on field work we had breakfast and then reported at eight in the square, where the farm manager would direct us to our various duties. Here he would give us lessons on tractor-driving. Although I became very familiar with the Fordson tractor, I never needed to drive it again. Later I would be dealing with horses not a tractor.

Field work was the hardest of all. It was the harvest. We worked until nine at night. We gathered wheat and oats and bound them by hand into sheaves, which we stooked about six to a stook. This allowed the air to penetrate and dry the corn. Our arms were scratched and bleeding with the coarse fresh straw and they nipped with the wet rain or dew. We tried to cover our arms with the long sleeves of our coat overalls, but it was no use. The sleeves got wet and stuck to our sore arms, so we just had to roll them up and get on with the job.

We were starving, not through lack of food but with hard work and fresh air. To begin with, the men would stop mid-morning for a break with a flask of tea and a sandwich. We had nothing – the first day. After that we cleared the breakfast table with anything that was left over and took our sandwich along. That was when I learned to enjoy bread with butter, cheese and marmalade – all laid on as thick as I could manage. There was no shortage of food because they made the butter and cheese and grew the veg. There was always the remains of a whole cheese on the sideboard. Actually agricultural workers were allocated an extra ration of cheese, but at Auchincruive that would have gone in one sandwich to take with us to the fields.

The matron in charge at the hostel where we were billeted had advised us not to go out in the evening at the beginning of our training, although we were free to do so. She need not have worried. Even at lunchtime back at the hostel, we flopped on our beds, hardly able to speak to one another … only hunger dragged us to our feet and to the dining room when the gang went for lunch. We even hurried with that, so as to stretch out for a few minutes more before going back to the fields until nine o'clock, because our evening meal was in the fields. A large hamper was brought to the fields to feed the men and ourselves.

This long afternoon and evening presented another problem. There were no toilet facilities! I do not know what others did, but I was quite ill on one occasion, only managing to get back in time at nine o'clock! There were five of us in my dormitory. I kept in touch with one girl for some years, but have since lost touch.

Having finished at Auchincruive I was posted to a farm in Biggar, South Lanarkshire. It was a dairy farm. The field work in progress at that time was potato-picking (howking, as we say in these parts) and shawing turnips, tops and tails. The latter was a tricky job, as you could lose fingers. I used my father's best kid gloves – the left hand that is – until the thumb hung off. After which I just had to take my chances, as by that time I was more experienced.

We milked at six before breakfast. There was another Land Girl, but she did housework in the morning. After breakfast it was my job to clean the dairy dishes: that is, all the pails, machines, etc., used in the milking. They were washed by hand using brass rods which cleared out the tubes of pieces of fat which often comes from the cow in the milk. After washing, the dishes were sterilised in a large oven. I was on my own and took a pride in the dairy.

When I finished in the dairy I joined the others on the tatties and turnips. We milked again at four and had our evening meal about six. I helped Annie, the other girl, with the dishes, after which we made a sandwich, and with a glass of delicious milk we retired to our room.

The room was a converted attic above the stable. The stair went up out of the kitchen. At the top was a small landing and from there you could see the horse. You could always hear him stamping his hooves. This was where, after the evening meal, we would read or write letters. I was never out of that room again until the next morning. Sometimes Annie would go into town.

One letter I wrote was to Miss Lander our representative. It was in reply to a letter from her outlining the rules and regulations. I had read that a milkmaid got a bit extra money. The pay for a Land Girl was £1.1s to you and £1.1s to the farmer. That is, if you happened to be living at home you would have had £2.2s. The milkmaid probably got 10/- ... I was delighted to point out to Miss Lander that I was a milkmaid and therefore would be happy to receive the extra money. This was very foolish, but I was very young. It was the farmer to whom I ought to have mentioned this. Miss Lander came and complimented me on the dairy – it had never looked so well. It was spotless and the rods which had been black were now shining gold. However, the farmer was not best pleased. He was not going to pay me an extra 10/-. So he took me off the second milking so that when the others went off at four to the milking I was left all by myself shawing turnips in the field; but then I finished at five and had the rest of the evening to myself. The farmer's excuse for this working arrangement was that he gave us inside work when it was raining. I had not noticed this myself.

I had not at this time received my full uniform. I had dunga-rees, hob-nail boots and gaiters. I wore my school trenchcoat in the fields and many times was soaked through.

There was another problem too. I felt that I would like a bath. There were no such things as showers. After working in the mud and rain, I had to wash off the boots and gaiters under a tap before I could loosen the straps in order to remove them. We washed in our room with a jug and basin. I asked if I might possibly have a bath and was told I could use the ploughman's bothy. The ploughman went to the Home Guard on Thursday night and I could use his bathroom. I did this once. It was one room and a bathroom. I bathed by torchlight, anxious all the time that the ploughman might come home. I could not do it again. The atmosphere was not comfortable since I had stopped being a dairymaid.

One day a coal lorry drove up and I was surprised to see one of my schoolmates in the Land Army uniform. 'You'll not stay here Ellanora,' she said. Apparently she had been working on the farm and had recently left. She had come in the family business coal lorry to collect her things. She did not stay long enough to give me her story and I never saw her again. She was right though – I soon made up my mind to leave.

I did not mind the work – I seemed to be able to take it in my stride. I was sent to wash down a cow which had calved and then to clean out a shed where the straw had become one with the floor and was alive with maggots when I disturbed it. Those jobs I was on my own and began to feel I had not been forgiven for my approach to Miss Lander.

We were allowed home once every two weeks for a weekend, at which time I was very glad to have a bath. We had our own home in Hamilton. Not very many people owned their own home in those days. On weekend leave I decided to look for another job. We had agricultural workers' employment 'books'. Unlike the forces, we could leave and be employed elsewhere. I advertised in the local paper for work as a Land Girl, but in the meantime I was sent by the Labour Exchange to write property tax notices in the bank building opposite the Food Offices where I had worked, and where the cattle still grazed on the surrounding grassland. I was to work there again some years later, but for now it was just a few weeks because my advert was answered and I went to work again as a Land Girl for a Captain Stewart at Barncluith. I was to work on the Barncluith estate for the rest of the war years, live at home and cycle to work.

Barncluith

Barncluith, the High Parks and Chatelherault were neighbouring estates in South Lanarkshire. The High Parks was known for its ancient white cattle. Chatelherault, which had been a resort of Edward VII when hunting, was reported to have been a copy of a French estate – a folly where the prince, as he was at the time, kept his dogs. I knew it as a ruin, not much more than a heap of stones.

Barncluith estate was beautiful. It was a modest stately home situated amid lawns surrounded by trellises supporting apples and pears, and screening the industrial area where the greenhouses and the market gardening contributed to the wartime effort. The driveway and gatehouse gave onto the Carlisle Road. The River Avon flowed alongside and the old mill was neighbour to the gatehouse, which was a gardener's cottage. Stones from the demolished Hamilton Palace had been used in the building of the many terraces that led down to the Avon. There was also a handsome tower house which overlooked the terraces and a little glass windowed 'court' house to the main terrace. The windows were scratched with initials engraved by diamonds, it was reported, of the lovers who had plighted their troth there.

I had been hired by Captain Stewart, but he no longer lived at Barncluith. The estate, which had been inherited by his wife Margaret Bishop, had been sold to one John Oswald Graham, and Captain Stewart had retired to a house in Miller Street adjacent to Barncluith Road. He had retained a couple of fields for market gardening, and a house and stable.

'How are you with horses?' he asked. I had no idea, but was willing to try. He showed me what to do, how to feed, bed and clean out the loose box. This was to be done twice daily and was his main concern, as sometimes he would not be there himself, and I was soon to learn that neither the gardener nor the boy helper would go near Dick [the horse]. Looking back, I realise I made no attempt to make friends with Dick, but perhaps it was just as well. I did not like the way he always seemed to show the whites of his eyes. Later, when more Land Girls came to work there, he took a bite out of Ellen's pullover. I used to cycle home for lunch and sometimes when I came back I would find the other girls waiting at the gate for me before venturing in, if Dick was loose in the field. I had a stick I used to keep at the gate with which to brandish and lead the others to the safety of the stable!

Ellen was another school mate of mine and when the head of the science department, 'Sister's right hand man', was to retire we had permission to attend that afternoon. When I got home, my father, who managed a shop in Hamilton, told me about this mad runaway horse which had crossed the length and breadth of the town before being caught by a soldier at the barracks! It had been Dick! Captain Stewart had been having his tea in the field. Dick, attached to the harrow, became impatient and bolted.

On the main part of Barncluith, Mr and Mrs Graham and Mr Graham's sister-in-law lived in the house. Mr Graham's mother occupied the lower house. Mr Graham's sister-in-law was also a Land Girl and worked alongside Land Girl Norah Wye *née* O'Shea. [We were known as the 'two Norahs' – she was Norah and I was Nora, short for Ellanora]. Pat O'Shea the gardener was Norah's father. Norah and her husband Fred lived in a cottage on the estate, and Pat lived with his wife in a house above the stables where he had brought up his family. Mrs

Graham's sister left to go with her husband who was an officer in the Navy, and Pat arranged for me to take her place ... so I left Captain Stewart, who now had another four Land Girls, and came to work on the main Barncluith estate which I so much admired.

[The estate] had two horses to be groomed, fed and worked. There was a little flock of sheep and of course chickens, as well as all the growing – tomatoes, cauliflowers, leeks, celery. Everything was bought in from seed in the greenhouses which originally had been orchid houses. As well as the market gardening, we cared for the terraces.

At the end of the War, I was looking to start a career of some kind. The 'Direction of Labour' meant that I was an agricultural worker and was meant to continue in agriculture, but there was no opening at that time to study for a career other than agricultural labourer – and so it was that once again I found myself temporarily writing property tax notices in the bank building opposite the Food Offices. When this work came to an end, some of us were sent for interview to the local HM Inspector of Taxes. This was the making of a career for me, but there would be many ups and downs before I eventually became a tax officer.

Elizabeth (Betty) C. Lowe
(*née* Wyllie)

Elizabeth was born on 21 October 1918 at Pittendynie Farm, owned and farmed by her father, Mr William Wyllie, in the parish of Moneydie, Luncarty, Perthshire. She presently lives in active retirement in Carnoustie.

AS a youngster I was very fond of animals in every shape and form and my one ambition in life was to be a veterinary surgeon. But my Dad wouldn't hear of it … he kept on insisting that being a vet was no job for a girl. Looking back now, he was probably quite right. In those days, there were no antibiotics or tranquillising injections for animals, and the patients had to be forcibly restrained before any treatments, or when operations were performed. It must have been a very tough life for both the animals and the vets.

So the next best thing was farming. If I couldn't treat sick animals, I could at least work with them – and I had it all worked out in my mind just what I was going to do when I had finished school.

However the best laid plans, etcetera … my Father died very suddenly in April 1936. Farming at that time was at a very low ebb, and with no son to follow on and only two teenage daughters in the family, my Mother was advised to sell up. If we could have known what was going to happen two and a half years later, things could have been so different; but there it was – the end of dream number two!

We moved to Carnoustie and after I finished school I got an

office job with Baxter Brothers [jute manufacturers] in Dundee. It was alright, but not exactly my cup of tea!

At the beginning of 1939, although everyone was praying that it wouldn't happen, it seemed more and more likely that there was going to be a war. A government pamphlet was issued showing the various jobs in which women would be needed, should the worst happen, and encouraging people to volunteer in the armed forces, nursing, munitions, factories, farming, forestry and other occupations. All of us young ones were madly patriotic and prepared to die (well almost) for our country, so as long as we had freedom of choice (that is, before conscription was introduced), like quite a lot of my friends, I joined up. You don't need three guesses to know where I signed on the dotted line ... Women's Land Army, of course. That was on the 3rd of February 1939.

In the summer of 1939 the powers that be decreed that all Women's Land Army Volunteers should be given a three-week training period. Now, I don't want to boast, but I did think that having been raised on a farm since birth, another three weeks were not going to teach me much more. By the same token, in only three weeks, girls from the inner cities were not going to learn a lot either. But I wasn't going to miss the chance of getting away from that office desk for a spell (with pay), so I persuaded two farmer friends to put up with me for ten days each.

After that, it was back to the office where we jogged along, getting slightly more jittery day by day, not knowing what the next news bulletin was going to announce.

Then one day, towards the end of August 1939, Gavin (he was one of my 'farming teachers') rang to say that one of his men had had a bad accident; it was the middle of harvest and he badly needed help. He was going to contact the Women's Land Army organiser to ask if I could be allocated to him and ten days after that war was declared. That was it. While not exactly in the firing line, I did feel that I was making some contribution to the war effort.

Dalcrue, Perthshire

Dalcrue was a large dairy farm near Perth and I lived in the farm-house with Gavin and his wife (who was my cousin). Milking was done by hand and there was a herd of one hundred Friesians tied up back to back, on each side of two byres. There were ten milkers, all female, divided into two groups of five and we started at half-three every morning. Group A took the left-hand side in the morning and the right-hand side in the afternoon, and vice versa for Group B. The first one took the first cow, and so on, and the first to finish her particular cow moved on to the next consecutive cow; for example, if No. 4 finished first, she went on to cow No. 6 – if you see what I mean!! Now, it didn't take long to find out which of the cows were the easy to milk ones and which were the ones with the nasty habits – nasty habits being (1) putting her foot in the pail, (2) kicking, (3) refusing to let her milk down, (4) swiping you around the head with a wet tail, and – probably worst of all – (5) obeying the call of nature while you were strategically placed on the milking stool. Con-sequently, as a result of this scientifically acquired knowledge, you stayed a little longer on the job in hand, as it were, if the next consecutive milk producer fell into any of these categories. In addition to these ten milkers, there was always someone on duty in the dairy to supervise the milk going over the cooler and into the ten-gallon churns. The afternoon milk stayed in the churns in the dairy overnight and was collected along with the morning lot at six o'clock by the Milk Marketing Board's lorry.

It was also the duty of the dairy person to see that the churns were filled with the correct amount. On one occasion, when I was on that shift, the Boss noticed in the mornings that the churns with the afternoon's milk in were short of the mark by about two inches. I was duly told to be more careful, but in spite of my meticulous checking the same thing kept happening for the next three or four mornings. The following night Gavin and I had to go out at two in the morning to help a cow with a difficult calving . We noticed smoke coming from the chimney in the bothy. We both thought it a bit odd that Archie, the sole occupant of the bothy, should be stoking his fire at that hour, so we started a bit of Agatha Christie stuff.

Gavin said that he was going to stay up all the following night and keep watch on the dairy. He did, but nothing happened. Two more nights like this and he was asleep on his feet, so I volunteered for the next night. The only room in the house with a window overlooking the dairy was the bathroom, so it was there that I took up my position. I didn't have long to wait as, about one-thirty, a shadowy figure came out of the bothy carrying a jug, disappeared into the dairy and came out again a few minutes later still carrying the jug. I woke Gavin and he phoned the police. They said that before they could do anything the culprit had to be caught red-handed, so the whole drama had to be repeated.

The next time we had success and Archie was caught in the act! A visit to the bothy next day revealed six milk bottles full of cream. It was not the quantity of milk stolen that was important, but of course it was the cream on the top of every ten gallons that was disappearing. Since the price of the milk depended on the butter fat content, this would have had quite a serious effect on the monthly cheque had it gone unnoticed. It appeared that Archie had a friend who was making butter and selling it on the black market – he was supplying her with cream.

At the beginning of March 1940 I got the shock of my life when I received a letter telling me that I was one of four Land Girls chosen to represent Scotland at a rally in London, where we were to meet the Queen. I think the best way to record this would be to include the letter here which I wrote to my Mother when I came back. It would be quite impossible for me to put into words now, the thrill and excitement felt by a young girl during that trip, especially a young girl who had led a sheltered life in the country and had never before been out of Scotland.

Dalcrue, Almondbank

March 1940

Dear Mum

Here I am again, back to old clothes and porridge after a simply marvellous time in London. It's going to be very difficult to give you all the news on paper ... it would be a lot easier to tell you personally. ... However, I'll do my best, so here goes!!!

Well, to begin with, Miss McLeod and Miss Lewis came out here on Friday 8th March and asked me if I would like to go to London to have the honour of meeting [Her Majesty] the Queen. I could hardly believe my ears! From then on until I left the following Wednesday, I went about in a blissful daze, absolutely seething with excitement. To make matters worse, I was sworn to secrecy and all the time I was bursting to tell everyone.

At last Wednesday morning arrived and I got up at 3.30 (not three o'clock as it said in the papers) and fed the cows and cleaned down the byre ready for milking, and still had time to milk two cows. Then I calmly informed the company that I had to go. (Mark you, I didn't say why or where!) They nearly threw a fit. After a hectic scramble, I got dressed and ready for the road by the time the taxi arrived for me at 5.45 (Gavin couldn't leave the milking) and I caught the 6.20 train for Edinburgh. That part of the journey was quite uneventful and I slept most of the way.

I arrived safely in Edinburgh at 8.00 and since I was not meeting the others till 9.30, I had breakfast at the Station Hotel. At 9.30 I went down to the London train where I met Miss McLeod, Sylvia Haig and Jenny Sloan. The fourth member of the group, Catherine Sinclair, joined us at Berwick. They were very nice girls – Jenny in particular was quite the most attractive girl I've ever met and very pretty too. The other two, although they had no special claims on good looks, were great fun, and after we had been on the train for about five minutes we felt as if we had known each other all our lives.

Well now, to get back to the scene on the platform – before we knew what was happening, dozens of reporters arrived and simply mobbed us. Two or three kept asking us different questions at the same time, while others clamoured for photographs. It was most exciting. We felt like film stars. At last we were allowed to get on the train, and not before time either for the guard was beginning to get quite annoyed.

We were very sedate until we reached Berwick and just told each other what our farms were like and what kind of work we did, etc., etc. Then at Berwick, Catherine joined us and the train filled up with soldiers. Four really nice ones came into our compartment and we all got very pally!! (Remember there's a war on and one can do things while in uniform that one wouldn't dream of doing in normal times!) But that's just by the way!! We had a most hilarious time all the way down and sang lustily most of the way. As a result we seemed to reach London very quickly, and after bidding our soldier friends good-bye we took a taxi to the Strand Palace Hotel.

When we arrived there, we washed and changed into frocks; then at eight o'clock four gentlemen – *viz* Mr Laird,[26] Head of the Department of Agriculture for Scotland, Mr Glen and Mr Kay (next to Mr Laird in the [Department]), and Mr Aglen, Private Secretary to the Secretary of State for Scotland – came for us and whisked us off in taxis to the Trocadero. First we had cocktails in the lounge – I had a White Lady! Then we went downstairs to the Grill Room where we had a most gorgeous dinner followed by dancing.

Our escorts were great fun. They said there were to be no formalities, so called us right away by our Christian names and insisted that we did the same to them, so immediately they became Pat, Alan, David and Jock (in the same order as above). At dinner, we had white wine to drink and finished up with liqueurs. This time I had a Benedictine. *Oh, boy!* It was marvellous. Then they took us back to the hotel at about 1.30 [in the morning]. Catherine and I both tumbled into our beds very tired, but very happy.

Thursday morning came round all too soon and the telephone beside my bed rang. I lifted the receiver and a voice all bright and breezy said, 'Good morning madam, it is now eight o'clock'. So I roused Catherine and we rang for a chambermaid to get our baths ready. After a lovely bath, we got into our uniforms and trooped down for breakfast en masse. What a sensation we caused in the dining room!

After a very excellent breakfast, we walked to the Scottish Office where we met Sir John Colville, Secretary of State for Scotland. He was very nice. It was he who suggested that since we had come so far, we should have another day in London. Jolly decent of him, wasn't it? Then he said that he would get tickets for us, for a show that night. He introduced us to Mr McNair Snadden[27] who took us down to the Houses of Parliament and showed us all round. We were in the House of Lords when a court case was being heard. When we came out again (about one and a half hours later) we found the taxis still waiting. Mr Snadden had forgotten to pay them. He had to fork out about twelve shillings. After we left him we had a snack lunch in the Brasserie in the Strand Corner House. Then we went back to the hotel, got tidied up a bit and then took a taxi to the Goldsmiths' Hall.

There we met all the others – up to a high doh like ourselves. We were lined up in fours, about 150 of us in all. I was at the top end of the second row. Round the walls were the lady members of the Department of Agriculture, like Miss McLeod, etc. We didn't have to wait very long before Her Majesty arrived. She was lovely ... dressed in royal blue velvet, frock and coat of the same material, coat trimmed with silver fox fur, blue hat and blue court shoes. She wore pearls and a most beautiful diamond clip in the shape of a maple leaf. When she stood in the doorway while the orchestra played the National Anthem, I felt like crying for some stupid reason, and I just felt that I would do anything for her. Then she walked up and down the lines and spoke to us – I tell you, I was fair in the jitters by this time, but once she started speaking to me I felt quite at ease. After she had inspected the lot, she had tea with us and then we gave her a Royal send-off.

After that we went back to the hotel to change and wait for our boy friends for that night. At that time we had no idea who they were to be, but at 7.45 they arrived. Jock and three others – R. L. Morris (whom we referred to all night as 'R. L.'), Sandy Main and Norman Graham.[28] I can't tell you exactly what their jobs were, but they were all 'high heid yins' in the Department of Agriculture. That night we all had dinner together in our hotel (preceded by gin and lime, of course), and after dinner we all bundled into taxis and whizzed off to the Hippodrome to see Black Velvet. And where do you think we sat? Nowhere else than in the Royal Box! All at the expense of Johnny (Secretary of State, you remember). It was a marvellous show and we all thoroughly enjoyed it. Don't think we went home after that. *No Sir.* The night was still young (11.45 pm), so we went to the Café de Paris Night Club. Boy, what a thrill! There we ate some queer sorts of dishes which I did not enjoy very much, danced, then ate again, and altogether had a high old time. Our escorts saw us back to the hotel where we just tumbled into bed. Not because we were the least under the influence, mind you, but just dead tired.

Friday we had entirely to ourselves, so we had a long lie followed by a leisurely breakfast, and then went out to see as much of London as possible in the time we had left. Miss McLeod knows the city well and she proved an excellent guide. I couldn't tell you all we saw, but just to mention a few – Buckingham Palace, St Paul's [Cathedral], Hyde Park, Marble Arch and Rotten Row. We went on a tube train for my special benefit, as I was the only one who had never been on one before. We had lunch at the Piccadilly Corner House and then continued our hike. This time we saw some of the shops – Harrods, Selfridges, etc. – but unfortunately we had no time to go in. After that it was tea at Piccadilly Corner House (you notice that we had a passion for Corner Houses!), then walked a bit farther before going back to the hotel to change for dinner – on our own this time, not so much fun but a super meal. Next it was a taxi to the Vaudeville Theatre to see 'Moonshine'. Another great show.

On Saturday morning we had to be up early to get our packing done and be at the station by 9.30 a.m. The train was very busy, but we managed to get a carriage to ourselves as far as York, then ever such a nice lot of soldiers and airmen came in – one of them had a wireless and we had great fun all the way to Edinburgh. Alan [a friend from Carnoustie] met the train at Newcastle and handed in a huge box of sweets. I only spoke to him for about five minutes and then we were off again, but he expects to get leave before long and I hope to see him then. At Edinburgh, Jenny's father was meeting her at the station and he saw me safely onto the Perth train. Harry [the local gamekeeper] met me with the car at Perth and brought me out here. He was terribly thrilled at having the honour of driving such a famous person, he said!!

There was great excitement here on Sunday morning. I was treated like a national hero. Everybody wanted to shake hands with me. It was great fun. I started this letter on Sunday and it is now Tuesday and it has been written at odd times in bed, in the boiler house and various other places. I only hope it makes sense. I simply couldn't finish it on Sunday night; all I wanted to do was sleep and sleep. It was the same yesterday, but I'm practically back to normal again today.

I think this is a fairly full report of the goings on. But I couldn't write this screed to everyone, so will you pass it onto the Aunties? – Kay, Uncle Tom and Auntie Meg – and anyone else who wants to know the details.

Write soon. Heaps and heaps of love,
B.

P.S. Please send on all the papers, etc., you have.
P.P.S. No definite word about Easter leave yet.

Dalcrue again

Mucking out a byre on a cold wet morning soon brought me down to earth and things jogged along as usual for a few weeks. Then I learnt that the casualty I was replacing was fit for work again and I was transferred. So after a few days leave with my Mum in Carnoustie I set out for Auchrannie.

Auchrannie, Perthshire

This was also a dairy farm, owned by a Mr Hunter and his sister, Miss Hunter. For convenience, I'll refer to them as William and Mary, but I never got around to calling them by their Christian names – that was not encouraged in those days.

William met me at Alyth railway station on what was a dark, wet, foggy day and we set off for the farm. About three miles out of Alyth, we turned off the main road on to a farm road, which seemed to me to go on for about ten miles. (In actual fact it was only about two, but we could do only about ten miles an hour because of the fog.) Eventually we arrived at the farm and the end of the road! I thought it must have been the last place on the face of God's Earth, and began to wonder how I was going to survive there.

Mary met me at the door and showed me to my quarters – a little room off the kitchen, with a stone floor covered only with a little bit of matting beside the bed. Certainly not a five star hotel, but adequate. But what finished me was the lovely little vase of flowers that was on the dressing table – I just sat on the bed and cried! But after a good night's sleep, I woke next morning to find that the fog had cleared, the sun was beginning to shine and things looked different altogether. It really was a lovely part of the country.

The workforce on this farm consisted of the Boss, a tractor man and his wife – called George and Isobel – another Women's Land Army [Girl] by the name of Alice who arrived after me,

89

and a young man called Davie. Davie, in today's terminology, would be described as having learning difficulties, whom we (very unkindly I'm ashamed to say) referred to as being 'only tenpence in the shillin''.

Our first job in the morning (more civilised start at this farm, half-five) was to get the herd into the byre and tied up ready for milking. Now, on a cold wet day they would be huddled at the field gate waiting for you to open it and let them get stuck into the food ... waiting for each one in her trough in the byre. But on a nice sunny day, they were not so anxious to oblige, and often chose to ignore my 'Sound of Music' yodelling which echoed across the meadow! And you could bet your bottom dollar that there was always one cow lying at the very far end of the field, which would not get up until I had walked right up to her.

Auchrannie boasted a milking machine. This was not very common at that time, and it certainly meant that fewer people were needed for the job. The milk went through a pipeline into the dairy, where it was cooled and then filled into one-third of a pint bottles, for delivery to schools, and one-pint cartons for private customers. There was no law about pasteurisation in those days, but the herd was very strictly tuberculin tested, and the milk was top quality and sold at a premium rate.

The Boss did all the retailing himself, so after we all had had breakfast, we loaded him up in his Austin 12 with everything but the driver's seat removed, and off he went, while Alice and I were left to cope with the more mundane tasks of washing and sterilising all the milking equipment and cleaning the byre.

I sometimes thought the milk round would be a nice change from pushing barrow loads of FYM [farm yard manure], but William wasn't at all keen on the idea of a swap! However, as a great favour on my day off, I was allowed to accompany him!! On those trips I took careful note of what he did and where he went and jotted it all down. Fate must have been having a hand in those goings on, because one morning, about six months later, Mary came rushing down to the byre in a terrible state and said that William was in great pain and quite unable to move out of bed. But, as they say in the theatre, the show must go on and the milk had to be delivered. Well you know who was there, ready and willing! Wasn't it a good job that I had made all those notes?

That was it really. William had very bad shingles and was out of action for about ten weeks. By that time I was well and truly into my stride and enjoying every minute of it. I've always enjoyed meeting and working with people, and since the customers seemed satisfied with the new milkman/maid, I was given the job.

The old car was beginning to show signs of wear and tear, so, with a little persuasion, William invested in a new van. This made the work a lot easier, for it was quite hard going man-handling crates of milk in and out of car doors. There were one or two occasions in winter when I had to dig myself out of snow and ice, but there were no major disasters.

And things continued thus for the next two and a half years. The work was hard and the hours were long, but we always seemed to have plenty of energy to dance on a Saturday night. There was a dance somewhere in the area every weekend, very often preceded by a whist drive. These were generally organised to raise money to send parcels to the troops, and were always well attended. I was persuaded to go to such an occasion the first weekend at the farm. I wasn't all that keen to go, thinking about the three miles each way on a bike, and that I wouldn't know anybody when I got there. However, there happened to be a very nice young man there who was tall and a superb dancer (two essential attributes in my book!), and I immediately decided that life at Auchrannie wasn't going to be so bad after all!

There was a large contingent of Polish troops in the area and some of them helped out on the farms at hay and harvest times. They also attended the local dances where they were very popular with the girls! When they wanted to dance, they would come up to a girl, bow, click their heels together and hold out a hand. This did not go down very well with the local lads, whose usual method was a jerk of the head and the question, 'Are you comin' up?' But there was no brawling. We had a lot of fun and made some good friends.

I think I should now mention that William's elderly uncle lived with them in the farmhouse. His name was Mr Tweedale and he was always referred to affectionately at 'Uncle Tweedle'. He was ninety-four years old when I arrived and quite a character. We found him one day standing in the middle of the yard, furiously ringing a large hand-bell. Everyone for miles around thought the Germans had landed! (We had been told that in the event of an invasion, the news would be spread by the ringing of church bells.) Fortunately, on this occasion there was no such disaster – it appeared that the bees had swarmed and Uncle Tweedle was just carrying out the correct procedure, which is to make a loud noise and the swarm will settle on some nearby tree or bush, and hopefully stay there until the bee-keeper recaptures them and returns them to a hive.

I mentioned Davie at the beginning of this piece on my time at Auchrannie. One day we had a bit of fun at his expense. Where money was concerned Davie was absolutely trustworthy, but chocolates, sweet things and cigarettes he could not resist and needed watching ... remember, all those things were rationed. I had brought a bottle of orange squash home with me from the town, and left it on the kitchen table. When we came out of the dining room after dinner time, it was half empty. Alice and I decided it was time for action and Davie had to be taught a lesson. 'Did you have a drink from that bottle?' we asked Davie. 'No,' he replied, with such an innocent look on his face. 'Oh, good,' I said, 'because that is the medicine for the sick cow.' There actually was a cow poorly that day. With that, Davie's face changed through a variety of shades of red, white and green. 'Well,' he said, 'I just had a wee taste of it ...' (half a bottle!) – 'D'ye think I'm gonna dee?' We assured him that he wasn't going to die, but it might be a good idea if the vet had a look at him when he came to see the cow.

Alice managed to waylay the vet before Davie did, and told him what was going on, and he agreed to go along with us (rotten lot, weren't we?) So when Davie rushed up to him and told him about the terrible 'mistake' he'd made, the vet said he would give him an injection same as the cow! Davie rolled up his sleeve and was quite prepared to submit to this enormous veterinary hypodermic needle, but the vet said that on second thoughts drinking lots of water would do just as well. (You see, were weren't that bad!) Davie spent the rest of that day with his head under the tap. Our chocolate and cigarettes were unmolested for a week or two – but old habits die hard!

We supplemented household rations with a bit of fish now and again. The river Isla ran through the farm and there was a mini waterfall known as the Slug of Auchrannie, which stopped some of the salmon going upstream. By going there after dark with a bicycle lamp and a gaff, we were able to land the odd fish. This of course was poaching and highly illegal and I hope I won't be prosecuted at this very late stage!

Craigeassie, Angus

Some time about the middle of 1942, I was given another posting, this time to an arable farm in Angus. The farm was Craigeassie and it was situated about six miles from the county town of Forfar. Here it was a completely different set up. This was a very posh place, and the farmer and his family lived in the 'Big Hoose' and he took no active part in the working farm. The staff consisted of MacKenzie the farm manager, Eck the foreman, Will the second man, Jim the third man, Stewart the cattleman, Smith the gardener and four Land Girls – Anne, Marion, Jessie and me.

We four girls shared one of the farm's several cottages and did for ourselves (self-catering, it would now be called!), and we all got on very well together. Marion and Anne, the quiet pair, teamed up, while Jessie and I were more kindred spirits who liked going out and having fun. We became good friends and remained so right up until 1998 when Jessie sadly died. Marion and Anne shared a bedroom; I had a tiny single room and Jessie's bed was in the kitchen. Consequently she was very cosy in the winter and nearly roasted alive in the summer! The cottage had electricity and an indoor toilet and washbasin, but no proper bath. To overcome this slight problem we had to fill a copper boiler situated in the back kitchen with cold water and then light a fire under it. When the water had reached the required temperature, we decanted it into the large tub which was strategically placed nearby. Thank goodness this piece of apparatus had a plughole and waste pipe leading to an outside drain, so we didn't have to empty it manually. Once a week, or maybe even sometimes twice a week, we went through this ritual and everybody had a bath (including the three single men in the bothy, who didn't have any such luxury in their establishment).

We took week about of being cook/housekeeper. When it was your week on, you were allowed to start work half an hour after yokin' time, and knock off half an hour before lowsin' time to prepare meals. (For the benefit of readers unfamiliar with such Scottish farming terminology, 'yokin' time' means starting time and 'lowsin' time' means finishing time!) We had our own ration books, of course, the same as everybody else, but we were so lucky being in the country as there was no queuing at shops ... the butcher, baker and grocer all had vans which came round regularly, and we had our own supply of milk, potatoes and eggs.

The first weekend after settling in and getting ourselves more or less organised, Jessie and I decided to explore the social scene in that part of the world. So on a Saturday evening we went along to the Justinhaugh Hotel, which was situated about a quarter of a mile from the farm. It was owned and run by a lady called Mary Ferrier. ... It was a really lovely little country pub, situated right on the banks of the South Esk river, hence very popular with fisherman. We introduced ourselves as the 'Land Girls at Craigeassie' and were warmly welcomed by Mary, who straightaway invited us to 'go through the beads'. The beads, forerunners to macramé and plastic, formed a curtain in an archway which separated Mary's private sitting room from the public area, and only those who were specially privileged were allowed access to the inner sanctum! We were enjoying our lemonade shandy when Mary reappeared with two young men. One of those young men was George, the local blacksmith, and he and Jessie took an instant fancy to each other – love at first sight, you might say – and, to cut a long story short, four years later they were married and lived happily together for the next fifty-two years until, as I said earlier, Jessie died in 1998. I can't remember what the other chap did or even his name – just shows how much interest he had in me, or I in him for that matter!

Craigeassie, being an arable farm, meant that the work varied throughout the year, and we Land Girls took part in whatever was going on at the time. Being farming bred, I was allowed to work with the horses and that was a real joy for me. There were eight lovely Clydesdales and they had always to be fed and watered before breakfast. Then there was a strict code of seniority amongst the horsemen – the foreman had always to take his pair out of the stable first, followed by the second man, and then the third, with the Women's Land Army bringing up the rear. The same was true in reverse when leaving the field. There was never any hassle ... nobody had to be reminded of the rules, and we all seemed to get into place quite naturally.

The traditional way to bring a pair of horses from the field back to the stable, was for the driver to sit sideways on the back of one horse and loop the reins of the second horse round a bit of harness on the first. Well, when in Rome .... I was doing just that, except I made the mistake of holding the reins of the second horse in my hand. Consequently, when that animal suddenly stopped to have a nibble at a tasty bit of roadside herbage, I made an unceremonious landing on my bottom, right at his feet! Luckily no damage was done and the only thing hurt was my pride!

When the potatoes were harvested, they were stored in pits

at the side of the field over the winter months. The pits were not as you might think, holes in the ground, but wedge-shaped clamps at ground level. The potatoes were first covered with a thick layer of wheat straw, and then another layer of soil. This kept them frost-free until spring. When the risk of frost was over, the pit was opened and the dresser put in position. The potatoes were then sorted out into three categories: (1) *seed* for next year's crop; (2) *ware*, i.e. bigger ones for human consumption; and (3) *brock*, fit only for animal feed.

Dressing potatoes in those days must have been one of the coldest jobs on the farm. It was alright for the man who shovelled the potatoes on to the dresser at one end, and the chap at the other end who manhandled the full sacks on to the trailer; but for the poor souls in between, who just had to stand there and pick out the rejects, it was perishing! With extra socks, gloves and even some hay stuffed inside your wellies, it still sometimes felt as if your fingers and feet were going to drop off! 'Piecey time', 'mid-yokin'', 'elevenies', call it what you like – it provided a very welcome break when we tucked into substantial sandwiches and had a hot drink from a thermos flask. The toilet was behind the nearest hedge, and of course you wouldn't expect to find any washing facilities in the middle of a field! But we always seemed to keep fit and healthy, and never suffered from any of those nasty bugs and bacteria which appear to be prevalent today.

If you've ever thought that harrowing a field behind a pair of horses on a beautiful spring day, with the sun shining and the birds singing, would be sheer bliss, then you ought to try it! After my first eight hours at that particular job, I was practically paralysed and the pain in my leg muscles was almost unbearable. Next morning, as I limped out to work, the foreman assured me – with a broad grin on his face – that the best cure was another day's harrowing ... I could have hit the sadist! Strangely enough, though, he was right, because as the second day progressed the pain gradually eased, but it was about a week before I was able to walk properly again.

Thinning neeps (as we Scottish country yokels call turnips) and sugar beet were jobs we all enjoyed, even if they were a bit back-breaking at times; but it was probably because there was always a gang of us, men and girls, and there was always plenty of chat going on. The men were much quicker on the job, and when they reached the end of their drills, they stopped for a breather to let us catch up … but as soon as we reached the headland, they immediately set off again – maddening, it was! But we weren't going to let them beat us and with practice we soon improved our speed.

We made hay and we made silage. When and how much was determined by the weather conditions at the time. They reckoned that if the pressure on the barometer was thirty [inches] or over, we were in for a spell of good weather, so haymaking went on apace. The grass was cut by a tractor-drawn mower, allowed to wilt for twenty-four hours, then turned over once, sometimes twice, by a horse-drawn implement known as a 'tumblin' tam', and dumped in heaps around the field. It was then built up around wooden tripods into small stacks ('ricks' or 'coles'), which were then tied down with ropes. In this state it was virtually weatherproof and suffered no damage from rain, so it was left in the field till it was a convenient time to load it on to carts and transport it to the barn at the farm. Good quality hay was a valuable food for the horses and cattle during the winter months.

Silage-making was not quite so dependent on the weather. The grass was cut the same as for hay, then loaded on to high-sided trailers and taken into the steading (i.e. the farm itself), where it was offloaded on to a machine which chopped it and blew it into a tower silo. Molasses [was] added at intervals to help the fermentation process. This also provided winter feed for the cattle.

Occasionally our workforce was supplemented by some Prisoners of War – Germans and Italians (not at the same time!) – and we got on quite well with them. There was no ill feeling, for we knew that they had been fighting for their countries just as our lads were doing for Britain. There were, of course, some language difficulties: for example, when on one very wet morning, the Boss said, 'Aw youse wi ileskins had oot tae the neeps, and youse without jist gang as weel'!! (Just in case the meaning isn't obvious, allow me to translate: 'All of you with oilskins take yourselves off to the turnips, and all of you without oilskins can just go along as well.')

Corn harvest was a particularly busy time, and we worked all the hours of daylight when the weather was right. A swath was cut by a man with a scythe at each end of the field to allow access for the tractor-drawn binder (no combine harvesters in those days). The binder cut the corn and bound it into sheaves and then dropped them on the ground. They were then picked up by hand and set in stooks – eight sheaves to a stook, in a sort of triangular formation which, one hoped, would withstand a certain amount of wind and weather, and remain thus until the moisture in the grain had dried sufficiently for storing. It was not unknown for some of the stooks to collapse if the weather had been exceptionally rough (or some of the builders not too expert at the job!?), and having to go into the fields again and set up wet stooks was positively the worst thing you could imagine. It didn't seem to matter what you wore, you finished up absolutely soaked to the skin!

When the conditions were right, the next stage was to load the sheaves onto a corn cart (a special flat cart with a rail front and back, and horse-drawn this time) and transport them back to the stackyard where they were built into stacks some twelve to fifteen feet high, then rising to a peak. This was a very skilled job and we Land Girls never mastered that art. In fact, I don't think we were encouraged to try. A mistake on our part would have been very expensive, not to say inconvenient, if the stack had collapsed in the middle of winter! Later on the stacks were thatched with wheat straw ... specially baled for that purpose. This straw was also used for covering the potato pits.

From time to time during the winter months, we did a day's threshing to provide food and bedding for the livestock – so once again we manhandled the sheaves. The thatch was removed from the top of the stack, the sheaves were loaded onto a cart and driven to the farmyard and strategically placed by the doors in the building which gave access to the threshing mill one storey up. A man stood at the head of the mill and as the sheaves were pitched up to him one at a time, he cut the twine which had bound them and lowered the loose stalks into the threshing machinery. The straw was carried on a conveyor belt to the end of the loft and the grain went down a chute into sacks on the ground floor.

Later on, the oats were put through a 'bruiser' ... a machine with rollers, which broke up and flattened the grain and made it suitable for food for the horses and cattle. Some of the wheat was treated likewise and fed to the poultry, and the rest of it went to the local flour mill. Any barley went to the maltings.

There was never a quiet time on the farm. As soon as the fields were cleared of one crop we had to start and prepare for the next one, and that meant ploughing. This was carried out with either a two-furrow plough behind a tractor, or a horse-drawn single furrow. Although this meant long days out in the fields on my own, I really enjoyed this work. Thanks to the expert guidance and patient tuition from Eck (the foreman), I achieved a reasonable standard – so much so, that I was persuaded to enter the local ploughing match. In a field of twelve tractor ploughs I was the only female competing ... to everyone's surprise – including my own – I won two first prizes and one second prize. Drinks all round in the pub that night!

Working with the animals was always a great pleasure for me and, from time to time over the six years, I acted as assistant midwife at the birth of calves and lambs. Sadly the calves had to be separated from their mothers a few days after they had been born, and bucket-fed, since the milk was all needed for human consumption.

Although we were all truly thankful when the War was over, I was sorry to leave the farm. However, I was fortunate to get a place at Aberdeen University to study – would you believe? – agriculture! We were a 'mature' bunch of young men and women, known as ASRIC – Association of Students Resuming Interrupted Careers! To fill in the time and also earn a little money before the term started, I worked in a cheese factory owned by the Milk Marketing Board for five months. This provided another interesting experience.

Those six years from 1939 to 1945 I spent in the Women's Land Army are an unforgettable part of my life. In the New Year's Honours List in 1946 I was very honoured and proud to receive the BEM [British Empire Medal].

Is it surprising that three years later I married a farmer?!

$$\Diamond$$

Una A. Stewart (*née* Marshall)

FIRST of all, I applied for an application form [to join the SWLA], and because I was just under 18, I had to get my grandmother to sign the permission form. A visit to my doctor for a health check completed the formalities. To be honest, I can't remember how my uniform arrived; it runs in my mind that I got it from the Land Army district officer for Angus after I was posted there. There was Miss Ireland from East Balmirmer who was over Miss Jackson, who looked after the Inverkeilor area. She was a lovely person who met me at Arbroath station on an absolutely freezing and very overcast day. Coming at that time from the mild west of Scotland, I felt the cold particularly badly. We drove six and a half miles to Ironshill Farm. Although very few people owned cars, especially in wartime, I was used to them – two of my uncles were doctors and they had one each.

Ironshill Farm

The farmer and his wife were pretty old. He was crippled with rheumatism. She was bitter because she had two sons who had fearful stammers of the mouth-gaping type. If you guessed what they were trying to say, it helped.

We drew up in the close at the back entrance to the house – no one uses the front door of a farmhouse. As we got out of the car, the byre door in the steading opened a little and three young men looked out to see the new Land Girl; the two farmer's sons, Douglas and Ian and Henry Edward Murray Stewart – the fore-man, horseman and my future husband.

That night Kate – the Land Girl who was leaving, the farmer's sons, Ed and I gathered round the kitchen range and Ed produced his button accordion. The farmer's wife produced a large bar of Cadbury's chocolate which I hadn't seen since before the War. We had four squares each. Ed put his on the side of the range where I watched it begin to melt as we sang songs of the day. I was too shy (don't laugh) to point it out to him and I was relieved when he spotted it before it was too late. About nine, the party broke up and we headed for the back door to see Ed off, opened it and discovered it was snow to the top! We dug him out and he set off home across the fields, because the road was up to the top of the telegraph poles in drifts. And so to bed.

Next morning a call came at quarter past four. I got up, put on my dressing gown, and set off across a huge expanse of polished linoleum (there was a lambskin rug at the bedside) to find my slippers, and, wash-bag and candle in my hand, made my way downstairs to the bathroom. The door consisted of two halves lengthways, with a bolt top and bottom. As I opened the right-hand side, somebody opened the back door and the draught crashed the door in my face and blew out the candle. As I stood in stygian blackness, the kitchen door opened and I was given another candle with the sharp remark, 'we don't bother with all that, Miss Marshall'! A freezing cold splash wakened me completely and it was out to the byre in double-quick time to make the acquaintance of thirty-odd cows and rather surly cattle-man. I quickly cottoned on to washing udders and clamping on milking machines. Kate was very helpful and showed me how to pull the dung into the grip, put in fresh straw and sluice down the cement centre walkway. In for breakfast. The farmer's wife had made a huge pot of porridge. The farmer, Kate and I had some with fresh milk. Very nice, but what happened to the rest? Was it for lunch? Or for tea? A row of bowls in the scullery (where we washed up cans and machines) was filled. Cold porridge for lunch and tea? My fears were dispelled at lunch time – a plate of soup with potatoes cooked in it and a bit of boiling beef.

At the end of the week, Kate and the farmer set off with her case in a horse and cart across the fields, taking down fences as they went because the road was filled with snow from side to side. They dug across the bridge over the railway halfway to the village. She eventually got to the station and arrived home safely in Dundee. I've never heard of her since. It was six weeks before we saw black ground. I cleaned out hen houses, tried to dig out leeks from the frozen ground and milked twice a day. Half a dozen of us walked six miles to Arbroath to go to the pictures and walked home again. Because of the weather, it was a walk to the village for a basket whist. In the basket there were sand-wiches, scones and cakes, all homemade, and china cups, saucers and plates, teaspoons, teapot, cream and sugar for four people. The farmer's wife chose not to walk to the whist. I was delegated to take her place. It was enjoyable once I got used to the game and the moving on [to a new] table after each game. The village hall was lit by Aladdin lamps and these had to be pumped up halfway through the evening. Boiling water was provided for the tea, boiled on a paraffin stove.

The weeks moved on through dung-spreading, potato-plant-ing, haymaking, harvest and always the dairy work twice a day. We arrived in November and I moved on to Kirkton Farm as cattleman.

Kirkton Farm

I didn't get away from cows altogether, as there were four to be cleaned out and left knee-deep in clean straw in time for a cottage wife who milked them at five in the morning to provide milk for farmhouse and cottages – they had four pints a day, a firlot of meal every month, and a load of potatoes in the autumn, which they preserved in a clamp in the garden covered by wheat straw and a spade depth of earth. Some had an allowance of pig meal for a pig in the sty behind the cottage, and some had grain for a few laying hens. I've forgotten to explain, the dogs got the bowls of cold porridge with fresh milk – their only food. The farmer's wife at Ironshill wasn't too pleased at my moving, but Miss Jackson fixed me up there, being billeted at a cottage which had no sanitation or electricity, but was clean and the food was good.

When the cattle were out in the summer, I joined the general work outside, being allocated the 'orra' [odd job] horse and cart. So I learned how to harness the 'canny' beast and do odd carting jobs.

Dressing potatoes was a new skill I learned here and that was a cold and dirty job. No one told you about the dirt before you joined, and the smell of rotten potatoes and dung could be added to that.

Talking about dung – the men plotted a test for the new Land Girl. They were emptying the cattle courts of the very 'ripe' dung which was taken out by horse and cart to be put in small heaps on stubble fields for us to spread later. To do this, they opened the pass between the courts and put a single plank over the opening. Now, I had to wheel a barrow like a small cart in size and heaped with turnips – a dead weight. I might have been quiet and reserved, but I had determination second to none, so I gritted my teeth, took a grip of the handles and started over. All the men leaned on their graips [forks] and watched. With all the care in the world, I placed one foot precisely in front of the other and, inch by inch, made my way over the plank. As I reached the other side, clapping broke out. My career as a Land Girl went up a notch.

All this time I had been with Ed – the first year at Ironshill. Every Friday we made for the village hall to a dance run by the Black Watch who were stationed locally for training. Mostly country dances, they included a couple of modern dances when only one or two couples went up. The band consisted of a mother on the piano, her son on the accordion, another on the drums, my boss at the Kirkton farm on the fiddle – and jolly good they were too. Saturday night was pictures night. You had to stand in a queue in those days, never mind the weather. Arbroath boasted three picture houses at that time. One was a bit of an 'itch and scratch', so we usually went to one of the other two. With the meagre sweet ration purchased, we settled down. Ed promptly went to sleep with his head on my shoulder, leaving me to enjoy the film.

We got engaged in November 1942. We went up to Dundee to buy the ring – an opal surrounded by pearls as it was the only one we could find that would fit my large size 'T' finger. Ed enjoyed no fewer than three ice-creams, two cones and one dessert at lunch. He's loved it all his life and still has it most days.

Drumbertnot Farm

I was moved to Drumbertnot Farm to general farm work in May 1943 and billeted with an RAF man's wife and small daughter. She was a very nice, gentle lady from the town, living out her time, while her husband served his country, in a cheap, damp, no-convenience cottage about four miles from Montrose ... she was glad of the extra money and company.

I spread dung for three weeks with an old man of nearly seventy at Drumbertnot, and the other incidents of note were cutting down and digging out the roots of a small wood to clear the land for cropping. It was very, very hard work. Harvest-time that year was very rainy and it was difficult getting the crop cut, stooked, carted and stacked. It was so slow that they had grubbed between the rows of stooks, and while turning the horse in the fields I received a kick from a Clydesdale through no fault of either me or the horse. They cross their front legs as they turn, and facing the head to turn him I stumbled on the clods of grubbed earth. His iron shoe caught the back of my ankle above the edge of my boot. I had the hugest foot with all the colours of the rainbow. Working on, I got back to the stackyard with my load to find the farmer, who was a bachelor, standing, hands on hips, looking exasperated. Two boys from the local Reformatory had been allocated to the farm to work. Every sheaf they were throwing up to the man at the pointed head of the stack was either going right over and back to the ground or out of the reach of the builder in his precarious position. It is a knack and they didn't have it. But I had. So, says the farmer, 'You'll do every stack and they will take the carts back and forward to the field'. This I did. I ended up exhausted, while they got a rest on every round, lying in the hedge eating a loaf off the grocer's van – bare. Not a happy memory!

Boddin Farm

At my request, when November term came round in 1943 I was moved to Boddin Farm, down at the cliffs and sea, a few miles from Montrose. Here I was back to dairying. The farmer and his wife made me welcome and I settled down to the routine. I rose, often in the middle of the night, to calving cows, and many a difficult birth brought a huge sense of achievement. When I went first the cows were milked out of old byres while a new one with all mod cons was being built. This meant the farmer could not sell the milk. He had built modern pig sheds with easy access for feeding and cleaning. Yes, kept properly, pigs are very clean animals. The milk for the most part was separated into cream and skimmed milk. This went to the pigs and I made 33 pounds of butter a week with the cream. As I didn't use a starter, my butter had no nippy taste but had a beautiful creamy flavour. A lot was used for baking and eating by friends and family and the local baker got quite a lot for his shortbread and cakes (including my one-tier wedding cake). I've no idea if any money changed hands. I was very happy here and made life-long friends with the family. I was married from here on 2nd December 1944.

We lived on a Chivers Farm[29] to start with and I learned a new skill with the fruit crop, raspberries and gooseberries. Later, still in the Land Army, although [our daughter] Audrey was on the way, we moved back to my first farm, Ironshill. Here Ed managed the outside work and men. When the War ended, I left the Land Army.

SPOKEN MEMORIES

The following memories are based on notes of interviews made by the editor. One – Margaret Watson – includes material subsequently written by the interviewee, and three – Anna Searson, Mona McLeod and Petrina Lithgow – incorporate parts of audio transcripts which were made for the exhibition 'Land Girls and Lumber Jills' held in Edinburgh in 2010.

$$\hat{\ominus}$$

Marion Allison (*née* MacMillan)

MARION left school at fourteen years of age and went to work at Templeton's carpet factory, Glasgow. She had started as a learner, then became a weaver before being called up on 13 April 1942. She already had one brother in the Navy and another in the Army.

Marion has no recollection of having to undergo a medical examination, nor of being measured for her uniform. [The uniform eventually arrived by post.] All items of uniform were provided free. She was not given a choice as to whether she wanted to be billeted on a farm or to go into a Women's Land Army hostel.

Marion was posted to a farm at Carluke at only one week's notice. She set off from Glasgow on the train at ten o'clock on a Monday morning, due into Carluke at quarter to twelve. Her mother saw her off and Marion recalls her saying, 'Mind and say your prayers'. She recalls being very nervous … this anxiety heightened by the fact that it wasn't a corridor train, so she nervously jumped into the first available compartment. … She wanted a compartment to herself so she could have a weep, but unfortunately, just before it set off, a man got into her compartment.

On arrival at Carluke, the farmer's wife was waiting to meet her at the station [to take her to the farm]. [Marion could not have foreseen that day] that she would be on this farm for nine years! Westerhouse Farm was run by Bill and Jessie Cullen; [Jessie was] 'a fine person and treated me like a daughter.'

As a Land Girl, Marion was an additional member of staff for Mr and Mrs Cullen, as there was no man there to be released for war service.

The day after arrival, Marion was set to work, hand-milking and carrying corn to the farmer who was using a sowing sheet. Her only training was [given] on the farm. She recalls being very [impressed] watching him, as he was like a machine working at such speed. Marion too sowed some corn, and when she saw it coming up the following year 'it strengthened [her] faith'. She also learned how to feed the hens, having to call out 'bird, bird, bird'.

For quite some time Marion was the only Land Girl on the farm, then a friend – Elsie Graham from Templeton's – was called up. Elsie's mother had gone to see Marion's mother to find out how to get her in to the SWLA.

Elsie joined Marion on the farm for about eighteen months, and they shared a lovely big room. Elsie eventually had to leave Westerhouse to nurse her husband who had been in the army and had been badly injured. He died shortly after the War. There was no replacement for Elsie.

The daily routine began with the milking of thirty cows at six o'clock and five [in the evening], so they were usually finished for six. Breakfast was served after the first milking, with the same thing every day on offer – porridge, tea, toast. Marion thinks Mr Cullen might have had a cooked breakfast. At about eight, when breakfast was finished, the milk dishes were washed. The next jobs [needing to be done] depended on the time of year. It could be out to the fields to sow turnips or shaw them.

Dinner was served at twelve noon prompt. The staff and the family ate together at the kitchen table – including the ploughman Jim Watt, who also stayed on the farm. Dinner was usually something like soup, mince and tatties, turnip, sago – Marion had not tasted sago before. She also tried tea without sugar for the first time too [and has not taken sugar since], as the sugar was needed for jam. They grew blackcurrants and raspberries on the farm, though the strawberries were bought in. Jessie made 365 jars of jam.

In the afternoons any sort of job that was required was done. Marion quite liked singling turnips, but she did not like spreading dung by fork. The farmer would leave 'castles' of dung and Marion had to fork it out.

The evening meal was served about half four before the evening milking. At about nine they would have supper of tea and toast. Marion recalls never being hungry.

There were two horses on the farm – Meg and Missi. Marion had to feed them when the ploughman was off. Missi was very aggressive so Marion would just drop her feed down in to her. Around 1943 Mr and Mrs Cullen got a 'red' tractor [possibly a Massey Harris or a David Brown]: this was in addition to the horses. Marion only drove the tractor once to 'have a shot', but she was too frightened to drive it and Mr Cullen didn't force her to do so.

Marion (and later Elsie) got every other weekend off. Mrs Cullen drove Marion to Carluke Cross to catch the mid-day bus to Rutherglen which arrived about two. She would be back in the afternoon on the Sunday. On one of her weekends off in 1944, she 'was home for [her] weekend when [her] young brother came in. He was in the RAF and was being moved to Scotland. Then [her] two older brothers came in … [they had] also been moved. Robert was a captain in the Argyll & Sutherland Highlanders. David was in the REME [Royal Electrical and Mechanical Engineers] as he was an electrical-mechanical engineer. [Her] mother was so happy to see [them] all in uniform, she wanted [them] to go up to Rutherglen Town Hall to meet [Marion's] Dad who had to work late at Provanmill Chemical Works.' Marion said later, 'You should have seen my Dad walking down the main street with the four of us in uniform. He was so proud of us.'

Marion very occasionally went to a dance at the Town Hall, but she did not attend too many. Mrs Cullen, however, was very fond of dancing. Marion herself liked doing a bit of knitting and attended the weekly whist drive held in a school hall in Kilncadzow.

Around 1942 every Monday Mr and Mrs Cullen went to the Hill of Westerhouse Farm to play cards. Jimmy, the eldest son of the house, played the accordion. One night in 1944, Jimmy starting singing to Marion, 'Who's taking you home tonight?' And it was Jimmy who walked her home that night, and later he was to become her husband. When they went into Glasgow to get an engagement ring (1947) there were only three trays in a big window display at the jewellers: one tray of engagement rings, one of wedding rings and one of watches. She chose a ring which cost, she thinks, about £80.

In 1944 additional help came along in the form of a German POW Hans Kehr. He was billeted at the POW camp at Carluke and came onto the farm daily. Marion was never discouraged from being friendly with Hans and in fact they stayed in touch for many years. When Hans and his two daughters visited Scotland years later they all had a meal at Marion's house. Hans died in Germany in 2007.

Marion served her time in the WLA on one farm; she wanted to stay because they were good to her. Mrs Cullen taught Marion to make pancakes, and so on, although she was not expected to undertake domestic work.

In 1945 Marion joined in with celebrations at the end of the War and led the Victory Parade in Carluke, representing the SWLA. She still recalls listening to radio reports about how the War was going, and feeling anxious about loved ones.

During the [severe] winter of 1947, they were snowed in for six days. Mr Cullen had to take the milk to where the snow was not so deep, to get the milk to a collection point for the distributor. That same year, Marion went to the first meeting of the Scottish Women's Rural Institute when it restarted after the War. This was at Kilncadzow. Jessie Cullen was voted in as President and Marion became the Secretary. Marion is still a member of the Allanton branch of the SWRI.

Marion recalls vividly the harvest of 1947. She and Mrs Cullen went off to their rooms to bed, whilst the men stayed down the stairs to play cards. Fortunately Marion slept with the door and windows open. She woke up at one in the morning gasping for breath. Smoke was pouring through the doorway. She jumped up and tried to get down the stairs [to warn the others], but it was impossible. ... Eventually Marion managed to wake Mr and Mrs Cullen, and only managed to escape the fire by jumping from a window. She woke the ploughman and Marion recalls that both he and Mr Cullen were in their shirt tails. Fortunately everyone was alright, but there was a lot of smoke and fire damage. Marion said her throat was sore for a long time afterwards, and later they found out that the fire was started by a cigarette [left] down the back of a chair.

After the War Mr and Mrs Cullen ran a bed and breakfast at the farmhouse. In 1952 Marion went along to help spring-clean the farmhouse ready for the season's visitors. Mrs Cullen had asked Marion to hang some curtains, but only if she wasn't pregnant. As it turned out, she was – so [Mrs Cullen] said she was not to climb up and hang them. She would do it. [Mrs Cullen] had been married fifteen years at this point and barely a month later she found out that she was pregnant herself!

Laura Bauld (*née* Lindsay)

FROM *c*1941-43, when fifteen to seventeen years old, Laura worked in munitions at Corstorphine, Edinburgh, but she did not like it. When the opportunity arose, she volunteered for the Scottish Women's Land Army and joined up on 2 February 1944. Her sister Jessie was already a member, and Laura recalls joining SWLA through her at the hostel at Midfield at Rosewell, East Lothian.

Miss Brockie, the SWLA supervisor, was a farmer's daughter and arranged for the issuing of Laura's uniform, including dungarees. There was no medical, as far as Laura can remember.

There were about eighty Land Girls at Midfield hostel. Laura shared a room with her sister and two others. Each day the girls were sent to farms around the area as needed, including Greenend at Gilmerton, Dalhousie Farm and Gourlaw Farm. Most of the time the Land Girls got a warm welcome from the farmers and Laura seemed to like all aspects of the farm work.

A list was put up on the notice board of the hostel on each Sunday evening, so that each girl knew where they were going for most of the week. Depending on which farm you were allocated to, the response might be 'oh, no!' – if, for example, the threshing mill was in – or 'okay, that's fine'.

Arrangements for lunches varied from farm to farm. On some farms, Laura was not allowed into the farmhouse, so she took shelter in one of the out-buildings. Lunch breaks would usually last about three-quarters of an hour.

At the hostel, when it came to the evening meal, the girls 'waited on the bell going for dinner ... went right down and joined the queue – it was at the back of five [o'clock]'. They ate in one big hall, all at one sitting. There was always soup, and meals like mince and tatties, sponge pudding or rice. The only choice was take it or leave it.

The hostel had a radio and a piano, but no record player. Laura remembers it was always fun in the evenings – usually someone among the girls could play the piano. On a Sunday evening there might be a garrison concert in Edinburgh, which the Land Girls could attend. Before the end of these concerts there would be an announcement to tell the girls that their bus was ready to leave.

The girls were supposed to be in by nine o'clock, with lights out between half nine and ten. If a person was late back after a dance, they threw stones at Laura's window so that she or one of the other girls in her room could let them in – Laura's bedroom was closest to the front door. The girls were not supposed to be in each others' rooms, so if they thought they were going to get caught they would hide in the wardrobe!

Laura's mum sent her a parcel every Wednesday, which contained things like homemade tablet and sweets. Letters and parcels would be laid out on a central table. The girls were always pleased when Laura got a parcel, knowing that she would share her mum's goodies with them.

Laura's four brothers all served in the Forces. John and Alistair in the Army, and Bill and Eric in the RAF.

Laura met William, her future husband, at Greenend Farm in 1948 – the same year she left the Land Army. (She was not made to leave the SWLA because she got married – it was her choice.)

William, born the same year as Laura, was a market gardener and had taken a temporary job at the farm. After the honeymoon they got a job together at Stow, Galashiels; Laura was the orrawoman and William the shepherd and dairyman. At the end of 1949 their first child was born at Stow and the family later moved to another part of the Penicuik estate, to Thornton Farm, Rosewell, where their second child was born.

Agnes Boyle (*née* Flucker)

AGNES lived in Newhaven and volunteered for the SWLA in 1943. She was interviewed and measured for her uniform in George Square, Edinburgh and had her medical on the same day.

Agnes recalls undertaking a four-week training period when she and the rest of the girls received eight shillings per week in wages. Mrs Gibson, who farmed at Pencaitland, was head of the SWLA East Lothian Region. Her deputy was Miss Weddel, who had a farm at Gifford. She came to pay the girls in cash in envelopes on a Friday night. When Agnes left the SWLA in October 1945, her wage has risen to 18/11 per week.

Throughout her service with the SWLA, Agnes undertook all sorts of work, which she enjoyed – although to varying degrees. She had experience of shawing turnips, lambing (though both of these jobs could be undertaken in extremely cold conditions), driving the tractors, working with livestock including horses, manual muck spreading (which always made her hungry), building the high ricks, and all manner of other farm work. She was never asked to undertake any domestic work, however; nor did she collect eggs or work with the hens.

Agnes met fellow Land Girl Ina Lithgow while working at Highlea Farm near Humbie, East Lothian. On her first day Ina recognised Agnes' face, and when she said her name they realised they had been at the same school. It was the start of what would become a life-long friendship. Agnes worked at Cauldshield Farm [East Lothian] for approximately three years.

During the summer, Ina and Agnes were billeted in a hut, not dissimilar to a Scout hut, in the woods in Humbie, East Lothian. Agnes recalls it having bunk-beds, a bathroom and kitchen. In the winter they stayed in the 'big house' that belonged to Colonel Peel in Gifford. This was his second home and was known as Eaglescairnie. There were twelve girls in the hut and sixteen in the 'big house'. The housekeeper, whose name was Mrs McLean, was known as 'Mrs Jimmy', after her husband ... the head gardener for Colonel Peel.

In spite of the regulations, the maid left the big window open for the girls so they could get back in if they'd been out late dancing. Ina and Agnes both recalled having the use of black Land Army bicycles, 'v. good bikes'.

A typical day was an early rise – approximately half four in the summer (a little later in winter) – a quick freshen up either in the bathroom or at the sink in the bedroom, where there was also a coal fire, then down to breakfast. Breakfast was laid out by the housekeeper and consisted of porridge, cereal and a cooked breakfast. You just helped yourself. Each girl was given a packed lunch, usually sandwiches, to take with her. Mrs Jimmy had the help of one person, Janet, who cycled up from the village (possibly Gifford).

A typical dinner was soup, and a main course of something like fish or mince. Mrs Jimmy was Colonel Peel's cook from the 'big house' and she was a 'lovely cook'. Agnes never remembered going hungry – food shortages didn't seem to have been part of the situation, although of course there were items that were rationed. All the girls handed over their ration books to Mrs Jimmy, as far as Agnes recalled.

A bath was taken in the evening, after the strenuous and sometimes not so fragrant work on the farm. There was one bathroom upstairs and one downstairs.

The whole group of girls [at the farm] got on well together, although of course there were inevitably a few ups and downs.

Entertainment took the form of dancing on a Friday night in the Goblin Ha', Gifford, or at East Saltoun. Music was often provided by a Polish band. The girls all wore civvies for dancing. Their partners were farm workers or even each other. They also went into Haddington twice a week where they went to the cinema, followed by a bag of chips ... and a sing-song on their way home. At weekends they finished work at lunchtime on Saturday and then most went back home, returning to the farm again at about six forty-five [on Sunday evening] to go back to Gifford.

Occasionally, Mrs Jimmy took them all off on a Saturday afternoon outing to North Berwick – 'Mrs Jimmy was so good'. Agnes felt that her efforts were always welcomed on the farms where she worked. There was a certain amount of respect shown to them when in uniform, although there could also be rivalry among some of the women workers.

Agnes enjoyed her time in the Land Army, but she also enjoyed going home at the weekends. She left the SWLA in October 1945.

Anna Searson (*née* Murray)

I WAS eighteen when I joined the Women's Land Army [in] 1941. I had quite a lot of girl friends away in the forces and it involved a lot of marching and I *hate* marching, and I preferred the open air and the countryside and the animals, so I joined the Land Army.

I served in Auchincruive at the agricultural college. I was sent there initially for a month's training. Well, that's a long story. There were 20 of us there and we were divided into groups. We did a week in dairy, a week in poultry, a week in agriculture and a week in market gardening, and at the end of that time we were called to the kitchens and the names were called out and the allocation where you had to go, and there were nineteen names called out to go to squads in Ayrshire, some to individual farms, and I was left. And I thought I was so stupid that nobody wanted me. So I was told to report to the office, and when I reported to the office they offered me a permanent job in the dairy there ... which I immediately accepted. I was there for the rest of the War.

The majority of girls who came [to Auchincruive] hadn't a clue – they were in the Land Army for the uniform and to be in the country.

... The worst job I had in all the time I was there was in the poultry division, because I did not like hens – I didn't like the smell of them, I didn't like their litter, I didn't like going up at ten o'clock at night to herd them in (in case the foxes got them), and I didn't like the way they pecked one another to death when they didn't like any particular bird – I really didn't like poultry. Wretched poultry, can't say I ever got on with them. The best job I had was in the dairy, I loved the milking, I loved the calves, I loved the cows and I was very lucky because the vet allowed me to stay with him when he was calving cattle, or injecting them, or anything to do with them. I thoroughly enjoyed dealing with them.

The food was adequate – plain but adequate – it was basic but very good, I was remarkably well fed – I don't say it was glamorous, basic but enough. ... The accommodation was a small [room] on the top of a house at Auchincruive. I expect it was the servants' quarters. I had a small room to myself and across the corridor was a small wash-hand basin, toilet and bath.

[I left at] the end of the War. When I left they offered me a post in Perthshire, a poultry farm, which I immediately turned down, and then they offered me a job in Dumfries to keep the records of the Ayrshire Cattle Society, because by then cattle were being registered. ... Really by then my parents were getting on and I felt I had to go home. So it was back to boring insurance.

I always had a love of the country and ... and I think really it opened my eyes to just how much went on on the farm.

Isabella Rankin (*née* Barker)

I FANCIED the Women's Land Army. I'd heard about the Timber Corps but wanted to be in the Land Army, so I volunteered. I went to an office at the back of [Edinburgh] Castle to enrol. Can't remember anything about the interview.

We were told uniforms hadn't arrived and we had to go to meet someone who would take us to the farmhouse on a farm in Pencaitland. I can't remember the name of the farm. We were also told to bring old clothes to work in. Us being townies didn't realise how old, old clothes had to be! I had black suede shoes on – we were all like that.

I had caught a bus from St Andrew Square. The farm was on an estate belonging to a big house. I had a couple of months' training on this farm.

Our second culture shock was when we asked where the toilets were! They laughed and said over the fence there and amongst the trees. For the first couple of months we were in a farmhouse, slept on these awful wooden bunks. Then we were moved to The Old Mill House, Pencaitland, away down a narrow lane off the Pencaitland Road. There were two of us here. The other girl was called Alice van de Peer. At the Old Mill house ... we had bunks with a biscuit mattress, no heating. The cooker was always warm though, solid fuel. The Mill House was a hostel holding sixteen girls, four per room in double bunks.

Suddenly we got a new housekeeper without any warning, never any gossip. We asked right out. The housekeeper was engaged to be married ... so we had a wonderful lady from South Africa. We were her family, she was super.

[Breakfast was] porridge, toast and stuff like that, eggs and bacon were rationed. When you think about what people eat now! There was no washing up done by any of the Land Girls (unlike the recent television series). We made our own packed lunches. I've seen beetroot sliced for a sandwich, or meat paste, just whatever was going. We made our own and we had an issued sandwich tin with a handle on the top, like a cash box only a bit deeper. Just water to drink ... the farmers never gave us anything. [Dinner] was always cooked for us, main meal and a pudding or soup and a main course. Things like sausage and mash, mince and potatoes and stuff like that. Steamed puddings and custard, just ordinary, like school food.

We always worked Saturday mornings; we made for home on Saturday after lunch. We had to be back by seven on Monday morning, so sometimes I would stay home until Monday morning but I'd have to get up at about four o'clock and leave about five-thirty. There were buses from St Andrew Square. I walked from home to St Andrew Square.

I left this farm after the harvest in 1943, though I still lived at the Mill House and then I worked at Dovecot Market Garden in Haddington. We thought it would be a change from harvest, but it wasn't, as it was harvest all the time. I still stayed at the Mill House, but worked at the market garden.

We had to knock the frost off the Brussels sprouts before you could pick them. It used to annoy me – the lorry drivers used to take fruit and veg into Market Street in Edinburgh, and the boys or whatever would just stand there while we lifted bags of about a hundredweight onto the lorry. They would just stand there shuffling things around. When you'd finished picking potatoes they had to go into a trench in the ground, lined with paper and straw – oh what are they called? – potato clamp. We did all the preparation for them. I got a go in a tractor once; I got to drive it because the farmer wanted something moving to the next field, another bloomin' field of potatoes!

[I used to get to work in a lorry] and the metal, oh the metal, oh deary me it was freezing! We had to go about five miles in this lorry and one day I said to the housekeeper, 'I'm on strike today until we get some sort of shelter on the back of that lorry because really it's unbearable'. I used to wear my grandmother's woollen combinations and if we were having a bit of fun I'd give the girls a look at them! So, I'd told the boss already the day before, 'I'm not going into work tomorrow. I don't know about the rest.' So I told the housekeeper I'd work in the house. I didn't want her to think I was going to sit on my backside. And then within weeks I did exactly the same until everyone of us had new Wellingtons because we were wet from morning till night, and we all got new Wellingtons so it was the twice I did housework. I helped prepare meals.

From the market garden I went to North Berwick about 1944. When I was eighteen I was engaged to a young man in the navy. We were engaged for about two years when I got a 'dear John' letter which just devastated me, and then the same week I had [an accident with a] pot of stew at home and burned my leg – [I was quite] badly [burned]. The Area Rep. came to see me to see if I was ready to go back to work; I said I didn't want to go back to the market garden. So I was posted to Quarry Court in North Berwick. It used to belong to a judge from Edinburgh. Because it was a holidaying place it was beautiful. [We lived at Quarry Court.] To my mind it was a different lot of girls all together; they'd had nannies and one of them, her father was the [Provost] of Musselburgh, and she used to run around in her brother's sports car. One of the girls went on to become a Writer to the Signet [WS].

I enjoyed Quarry Court – we had dates with everybody – Polish lads, army boys, RAF, invitations everywhere. I didn't go home every weekend then. We had great fun there, it was wonderful. There was a pretty girl, Ella, she had the most fabulous smooth creamy skin, she really was lovely, her eyebrows were as if they were painted on. Her and the boss's son rowed everyday for about three weeks and then they fell into each other's arms. Eventually they got married and had a son less than a year later. She was keeping house so had left the Land Army, and of course she couldn't go into the fields anymore.

There was a NAAFI [Navy, Army and Air Force Institutes] on the ground floor [of Haddington town hall], a café, and upstairs was the local hop. After harvest I had a big do at the hall – think it might have been in Saltoun. The main drink was cider. I didn't drink but I wanted to, and went to town on the cider and giggled all the way home.

I was the youngest and got kinda babied. I had a good time at Quarry Court. We got invites from everywhere all over East Lothian – Army Messes, Officers' Messes – and one night I said I'd like to go to the do with the Naval Air Corps but I was outvoted so we went to the Sergeants' Mess at East Fortune and that's where I met Alex. He asked me to marry him within twenty-four hours of meeting him. I said, 'But I don't know you'. We married about two years later.

An RAF plane flew right over our heads [once], smoking. It flew on and then we heard it crash and we were all sad for the rest of the day. The only other time was when the Germans were going over wave after wave for hours on end for Clydebank, and then silence. I had an uncle at Dunkirk, he survived that and then was sent to Italy later. Another uncle was in the AFS [Auxiliary Fire Service]. I was the only niece or nephew who wrote to him on a regular basis. And my brother was in the Royal Scots. When things were bad, you sort of worried for them. There were some POWs but we weren't allowed to mix – the owner wouldn't allow it. He didn't even let us fraternise with the local women.

In the daytime [I sometimes wished I had not joined]. I liked it best at night. Your legs used to give out on you. We had fun together [at night]. We were fed and we were warm. Had great fun really; we'd all be fed and the new housekeeper would make tablet for us – don't ask me where she got the sugar, or the toffee apples!

I felt I'd had enough [by the end of the War]. It was an Area

Rep. who came to us and said the town needs nursery nurses and three of us from Quarry Court said yes, we were interested. 'Well you only get £5 per month,' she said. It was usually ministers' daughters and the like, this was just the hoi polloi coming in, 'but we'll give you matching funding from the Benevolent Fund', she said.

The best [thing about being a Land Girl] was the camaraderie in the hostel; the worst [was] the winter weather, plus the fact that we were expected [to do], and did, heavier work than the men and us just little city girls with no muscles. Mind you, we soon developed them!

Mona McLeod

I JOINED the Land Army in July 1940, a few weeks after Dunkirk. When War broke out I was only sixteen and a half and I had just matriculated; [this] gave me an entrance to universities, but not to Oxford and Cambridge, and I'd got my eye set on Cambridge.

My grandmother and my two younger sisters and I were evacuated to a cottage in the Yorkshire Dales, and shortly after Dunkirk my father came out to see us and he said, 'Mona, I want to speak to you.' So I said, 'Yes Daddy'. He called me into his study: when he did this it usually meant we were in trouble. On this occasion, however, he said, 'I believe as I always have done in the importance of the higher education of women', and I said, 'Yes, Daddy', and he said, 'but I think we ought to concentrate on winning the War'. So I said, 'Yes, Daddy'. He said, 'So I've arranged that you could join the Women's Land Army [WLA] … I had arranged that you should go to the University Farm (this was Leeds University), but I've discovered that the RAF has got camps all round the farm, so I don't think it would be a very good idea. So I spoke to the farm manager's wife [who happened to have been my Guide Captain] and she has spoken to her father, who's a farmer in Galloway, so I've arranged that you should go and work for Mr Armstrong' – and a fortnight later I found myself either making hay, or if it rained, as it often did, cutting thistles. An extraordinary thing is, it was years after before I thought what an extraordinary situation, where my father had decided what I should do without asking me.

I felt quite excited about it. I had been to the farm in Galloway when I was a Girl Guide in 1938. Our Guide Captain, the daughter of the farmer, had taken us there, so I did know the family.

[My uniform consisted of] short-sleeved shirts, one jumper, one pair of ill-fitting breeches, three pairs of woollen knee-length stockings, one pair of leather boots and a pair of wellie boots, two pairs of dungarees, one short cotton coat, one rain-coat, one hat, one tie and badge. Items of uniform could be replaced annually if they were worn out. After about three years we got a very nice coat, well-cut but impossible to work in. For any girl working out of doors in all weathers, the uniform was grossly inadequate. Women in the armed services had protective clothing; we did not. In my first winter I had chilblains on my ears, hands, knees and feet. The turnips I had to pull and shaw were often covered in ice; if you did wear gloves they were rapidly soaked. Wearing my brother's cast-off tweed jacket or battle-dress top and the gloves, waterproof leggings, woollen long-johns and clogs which I had to buy, I discovered in my second winter that it was possible to keep warm in all but the hardest conditions. The clogs were a wonderful discovery. When lined with straw which had been heated over the boiler in the dairy, they kept your feet warm and dry all day. I have no memory of an arm band and certainly received no triangles.

The uniform was returned [at the end of service], but not the boots. I still had the boots when I joined the Edinburgh University Climbing Club. I'm still a member of the Ladies Scottish Climbing Club; I've been a member for forty years.

I served in the Land Army in Galloway for five years. I didn't see another Land Girl for about nine months. Mrs Grierson, the Area Supervisor, organised a tea-party for all the Land Girls in Galloway – there would be about twelve girls. The first year I lived in the farmhouse with the old farmer and his wife, and after about a year he had a stroke and I moved down to live with the farmer's son who farmed the neighbouring farm. He and his wife had been fairly recently married and it must have been an appalling situation for them, having this brash seventeen and a half year old Land Girl – oh no, I was eighteen and half by that time – coming to live with them. I never asked to go anywhere else; it didn't feel appropriate.

I found it difficult because they treated me as one of the family, and I felt that to go and sit in my bedroom in the evening and read would be rather impolite; and so instead, having come in from work about six o'clock, I had my supper in the kitchen, boiled a kettle of water in order to wash (as there was no hot water by that time), went upstairs and changed, then came down and sat in the corner of their sitting-room reading my book. I subscribed to the *New Statesman*. Penguins were only 6d so I could afford to buy them. I always kept a Penguin book in my pocket, even if only to read it for three or four minutes at a time. I think I was useful to them because I occasionally babysat for them, but otherwise, looking back, I think how very hard it must have been for them.

I felt torn about staying in my room, wanting to read (during the summer at least; it was too cold in the winter). I thought it was rude not to spend time with them. They went to bed about nine o'clock when the fire was going out and I went to bed about ten o'clock. Now, looking back, it seems tactless staying with a young couple. Once when they went away for a week I looked after the baby – it was a pleasant change from the farmwork.

When I started they tried me out in the dairy. It was a very big farm with about sixty cows – Ayrshires – and they made a very good cheese, a Cheddar type. … The herd was milked with machines, but there always were a few cows who wouldn't let down their milk and they put me on to milking cows. Well, after a week it was perfectly clear that every cow I touched went dry almost immediately, so they took me away from the cows and they put me on to the horses where I got on very much better. So basically I became the odd-horsewoman. I had one horse; mostly the men worked with two horses and I did a lot of carting, harrowing – the simpler jobs. I did occasionally hold a plough and pretend I was ploughing with two horses, but I was certainly not a ploughwoman.

Jobs I really hated were ones like shawing, shawing turnips when there was ice on the leaves of the turnips – your hands got absolutely frozen – singling turnips was a ghastly job, ten hours walking up and down, trying to get a thick row of turnips to one single turnip to every five inches. The whole squad came out, all the men on the farm came out to do this; it was deadly boring and I was very, very bad at it.

The work I enjoyed most really was with the animals. My father knew when he decided to send me into the Land Army, I loved animals, I loved the country, I loved farms and I was very strong, and so I was really trying to prove to the farmer in particular, and the men in general, that I could do almost anything a man could do – but I couldn't. I couldn't, for example, sharpen a scythe and most of the men were extremely generous, kind and helped me, taught me all the things they could.

… What for me was a complete morning off [was] when I was asked to take the horses to the smiddy to get them shod. This happened about once a month. The smiddy was about four miles away, so eight miles walking, usually with three horses, and when I got there the blacksmith's wife always gave me a cup of tea and scone.

I started work at seven o'clock. I got up at six and had a proper breakfast, porridge, eggs, bacon and scones. We worked from seven until twelve noon, had until one o'clock for lunch and then worked until six. It got terribly cold though.

As [the tractor had] an iron seat and no cushion, you got a sore bottom going up and down the drill and there was no cover [i.e. no cab on the tractor].

The work I loved best was working with the shepherd with the animals, or dipping sheep or clipping. I can clip. I never learned how to work a dog, but I would have liked to have done. [Other duties included] hedging, ditching, mending stone dykes, cutting thistles, we used a heuk and a scythe, spreading dung.

Liming was awful, you sweated and then the lime would stick to your face. It burned and the same happened to your hands if you didn't have gloves on. [Unloading lorries] was very hard on your back.

I didn't notice the time when I worked with the animals, whereas if I was hoeing a row of turnips I used to think, 'don't look at your watch until you've got to the end of the row'.

I always liked the mill day, a steam threshing mill, it was fun. I was terrified of rats. If there was a man there I would always try to kill them, but if not I would just wait until they had gone away. But on a mill day I found I got a blood lust, the more I killed the more I wanted to kill. I was quite shocked to find this.

For the first month the Government paid the farmer to train the Land Girls at a rate of 10/6 a week. After that the farmer paid the Land Girls' wage, you got your keep and 12/6 a week. By my fifth year I was being paid 32/6, well over the minimum wage, but less than a single man would have got. Married men, often highly skilled, were being paid £3, less 5/- for a two-roomed cottage with neither electricity nor running water. For overtime I was paid 10d an hour. If the weather were suitable during the six weeks of hay and harvest, we had to work all Saturday afternoon without extra pay.

We got one paid holiday and one travel warrant a year and I asked for one unpaid holiday a year at Christmas. We didn't get any breaks. If you worked overtime this was until [eight at night] ... and the farmer's wife would bring over scones and tea. On top of a ten-hour day, it left me without the energy to do anything but eat, wash and go to bed.

In 1944 my younger sister Mary joined the WLA. It was wonderful to have her company at weekends. She worked for an admiral's widow who had a goat farm at Skyreburn, about four miles from my farm at Townhead. The house was full of books. I enjoyed both her books and her conversation, too often limited in the farming community to prices and the weather.

We sometimes went to whist drives, but joined the tables reserved for beetle drivers. These were held in Gatehouse of Fleet, always on nights when there was a full moon and cycling or walking in the black-out was less dangerous. There was a Forces' canteen in Kirkcudbright to serve airmen from a rescue station. Land Girls in uniform were welcomed.

I joined the Scottish Women's Rural Institute at Gatehouse of Fleet. The first time I had to give a vote of thanks I was shaking like a leaf. We met once a month. I did not enter the competitions – typically 'the quickest potato peeled' or 'how many things can you get into a match box'.

I met my first husband on a mill day. He was waiting to be called up. Norman ran me back on his motor bike from Littleton Farm [another family farm] to Culreoch, Gatehouse of Fleet. The family was called Armstrong; the other main farming families in Galloway were the Griersons and the Grahams.

Sunday I would go out on my bike. Saturday I might go to Kirkcudbright and Sunday to the coast, Solway Firth – Borgue shore – in summer I might go for a swim. If possible I would ride [a horse].

[I heard news of the War] partly because my father's letters brought me news of my brothers and sisters [some of whom were serving in the forces]. I just heard the bombing of Clydeside, I never was in any kind of air raid. We worked with Italian prisoners of war; they would sing arias from operas. They had a ration of dried fruit. I was twenty-one during the War and I think we swapped cigarettes and dried fruit. I sent it home to make a cake.

The Land Army opened up a whole new world for me. The long-term effect of this was a wonderful escape from the very narrow life in which I had been brought up. [Ours had been a] very academic household where all your ideas were at least focused on what was going on in the world, international affairs and a future as an academic. I think I learned to value people in their own right. I certainly benefited enormously from being very well fed for five years, and also from having very hard work and a lot of exercise, which has stood me in very good stead.

When the War ended ... I had volunteered to go abroad to do relief work in parts that had been occupied by the Germans, but when I got in touch with the organisation – the Girl Guides were organising this – they said I was too young to be sent abroad. ... Since I had a place waiting for me at Edinburgh University, which my father had secured before he made all these arrangements about me joining the Land Army, I was given immediate release and in September I left the farm and went to Edinburgh University where I studied history and fine art. ... Looking back, I'm grateful for my period in the Land Army, but I wish it had been for three years rather than for five.

Margaret Watson (*née* Macbeth)

I WAS working in a grocer's shop. I left school at fourteen years old, and my parents paid for me to go to college for a commercial course, after which I worked in a builders/joiners office. I worked there for a few months then mother took ill and I had to leave to help at home. I was earning the least, so I was expendable! After mother was well I didn't feel like going back to the office work, so went to the labour exchange, as it was then, and got the job at Massey's the grocer at Scotstoun. It was while I was standing behind the counter a tram stopped outside the shop and I looked up to the top deck and there was a girl in Land Army uniform. I knew the girl because we were at primary school together. In fact, she and I shared the top place all through to qualifying class. I never saw her from then until that day on the 3rd September 1948. I just knew that it was what I wanted to do. There and then I asked the boss, Mr Henderson, if I could have the phone book, looked up the number of the WLA office in Bath Street and was allowed to make the call. An interview was arranged to fit in with the half-day holiday, then a medical was arranged. I passed the medical and my measurements were taken for my uniform, but I had to get my parents to sign my enrolment form as I was under eighteen, and they refused at first till they saw I was determined to go.

There was no training given and [I] was lettered with my train fare and destination. And so it was on the 30th September 1948 I got off the train at Abington Station where a hire car and driver were waiting to take me to the farm where my new life was going to begin. The farm was Greenfield Farm, Crawfordjohn, and the tenants were Jack and Jessie Thomson and ten-month old Kathleen.

They showed me to my room, which was one of the four bedrooms in the house, this was where I was introduced to my uniform and workwear. The room was very comfortably furnished, but getting used to paraffin lamps (electricity hadn't reached Crawfordjohn then) ... Jack and Jessie were very generous with food. There were no other Land Girls on the farm or in the area; the ones that had been there left when War ended, I was told. I got time off (between milking times), Saturday and Sunday, and got a weekend off every month, Saturday morning to Sunday night. I had to be taken to get a train at Abington to Lanark, get a bus to Glasgow, then another bus home, in all about three hours, and the same in reverse to get back on the Sunday.

I never saw anybody from the WLA; if there was a supervisor I never met her. It was harvest time when I arrived and the crop was already cut in the field. My first inside job was being introduced to the cows and given a luggie and a stool and sat down at the cow! Managed it though.

Outside it was setting up stooks, my first task in the field; there was Andrew, who was fifteen years old, so I more or less had to do what he was doing, and it was horse and cart work, then forking the stooks up to the builder on the cart to take it to the stacker. So a typical day started with the milking, then mucking, then field work and ended with milking.

I was treated like one of the family and fitted in very well. I really was sorry when they said they were leaving the farm on the 28th March because the estate would not do the repairs Jack wanted. So I had then to contact the WLA to see if they could get me another placement and it was to McBrayne's Market Garden at Canniesburn on the Milngavie Road. This was a very busy work place. There were three other Land Girls there – two Helens and another Margaret – head gardener, foreman and about a dozen labourers, and over the seasons, students. I enjoyed my time there, but I couldn't live on the pay. As I was living at home I had to give my mother half my pay and then I had travel expenses; it took two buses both ways. I hired a bike from the WLA at one shilling a week, but that wasn't all that successful. So I decided to ask for a transfer to a live-in farm.

Luckily they had one at Boghouse Farm, Crawfordjohn – tenants, John and Sarah Young. I took my bike with me, it was very handy there. The Youngs (and the Thomsons) were tenants of the Douglas and Angus Estates, as were most farms in the area. Boghouse Farm was a dairy farm and had twenty-seven milk cows, one bull, one horse, three hen houses and relevant number of hens. My typical day here started with getting the cattle in ready to start the milking at six o'clock. Mrs Young's hands were quite deformed with arthritis, but she could manage to put the milk machine on the cow and I took care of any hand-milking. There was three milk machines and [I] lifted them out when they were full and carried the milk to the cooler. We had to have the churns filled, for the lorry came to uplift them at seven forty-five in the morning. The beasts were put back out, then the byre was mucked and then in for breakfast.

[There were no little luxuries], no cream off the top of the milk here! [The porridge] was reheated and mostly stuck to the bottom of the pot, so the burnt bits were stirred through it – but when you are hungry there was no alternative! After porridge we had a slice of roasted cheese so that helped a lot. When finished it was out to feed the hens and collect any eggs, then I did the milk dishes and churns and cleaned out the dairy. By that time it was time for a cup of tea and my one biscuit, then I peeled the potatoes as Mrs Young couldn't because of her hands. Back out to do whatever was next. Sometimes I had to yoke the horse and walk up the road to the top field to hurkle the potatoes. (The hurkle was a plough for setting up the drills, drawn by the horse and steered with the reins attached to the handles.) One time I got up there to find some of the young herds had been busy and had lifted the hurkle up onto the dyke [for a practical joke]. I had quite a struggle getting it down without demolishing the dry-stane dyke!

This was generally how life went on at Boghouse Farm from 1949 to 1952 when I broke my wrist going through barbed wire on my bike. This was Mr Young's fault so not a lot was said about it. Anyway with my wrist in plaster I was no use, so they hired a byreman and his wife and they moved into the cottage and they did what I had been doing. When I got my plaster off I put in my notice, as I could hardly put a man and wife out of work.

It was at this point George – who used to come to the farm to buy cream for his aunt – took a part in my future. (George was a farmer's son. His father had died in 1945, so George was looking after his uncle's farm in Crawfordjohn.) By this time he was working as farm manager at Glendouran Farm, owned by Major and Mrs James Taylor. George told Mrs Taylor I was leaving Boghouse Farm and she asked if she could have first chance of me. So I went to work there alongside George. [Although the Land Army was disbanded in 1950, Margaret continued to work at Bog House Farm until 1952. George and Margaret were married in 1955.] I had five very happy years working for the Taylors, only leaving when the Major died and Mrs Taylor gave up the farm and went to live in Dorset.

Petrina (Ina) Lithgow (*née* Seaton)

WELL, in these days ... I was called up in 1943. I was twenty-one at the time and we were asked what we wanted to be in; and I said the Land Army ... and I just got in in time, seemingly, and after that it was the forestry, and after that it was killing rats on the farm, so I wouldnae have liked that.

I never really thought about [joining anything else]. When we were asked [where] you wanted, you went up when you were twenty-one and you were asked what you wanted to be in and they were telling us there was the Navy and ... and then he come to the Land Army and the Forestry and I said well ... I could work on a farm, but there was no way if you were living down at the docks and you were working in a biscuit factory, you know.

Well, there was a Land Army in the First World War and it was disbanded after it was finished, and they did the same for the Second World War to let the men get away to be in the Forces ... It left the women [to get] ... work [in] the Land Army and it was great – most of us enjoyed it. Really was nice, working out in the open air and knowing that you were helping the war effort in your own way. Didnae seem much, but it was a big help and it was great. So I lasted right through the War until 1945.

Well I put my name down for the Land Army. I didnae know if I would get into it or not, and we went up to George Square in Edinburgh and in these days your mother went with you – you know nowadays they want to go everywhere themselves, they dinnae need an escort. My mother said, I'm getting dressed and I'm coming up with you. So she went up with me, and we went up to a nice room in this lovely square and you were asked what you wanted to be in and I said the Land Army, and she said, right, we're getting kinda filled up now, but she says, we'll see what we can do. She asked if I'd ever worked on a farm or anything like that before, and I says no but I like the fresh air and the open air and we used to go to caravans and things like that, so you were in the open air then anyway. And they said that we would get notice and I got notice when I went home, on 6th June and I was getting sent to Humbie and to a Mr Reid's farm at Highlea, and they said I was to get on the bus at St Andrew Square.

We got to St Andrew Square and there was a bus at quarter to seven and it took us right through on the Sunday ... I think it was the Sunday. And Mrs Gibson from, oh I cannae mind the name of the place, it was somewhere in East Lothian, and she came and there was quite a few of us to go in her car and she took us out to the ... it was a hut and there was twelve people could sleep in it. ... And there was a place for the leader, see, and she was a Mrs Morrison and she always had a dog with her and that was a help as well – it kinda broke the ice a wee bit. And we went in and there was like a big dormitory ... six beds on each side, twelve of us ... and there was big boxes in a corner ... we were told to go in and all the uniforms were in the boxes in the corner and you were to go through each box till you got your own. ... So it was quite a laugh because sometimes you picked one that was too small and you had one too big, and then it come to the boots and the shoes as well and you got the whole uniform.

[The uniform] was absolutely beautiful – everything was lovely, the jumpers and the shirts, they were creamy shirts, green pullovers and a nice short jacket and lovely shoes, the good name that was then, way back in the 1940s, and then we all had our own sizes and everything and it was lovely. And then you picked your bed. Mrs Morrison was a good cook and a good ... she run a good house.

I expected, when I went, to work with animals and things like that, and no be out in the fields at all – always thought that was men's work – but no, we all strode out into the fields and got on with it and did as we were told and it was super. We didn't work with the cows ... or anything like that – you could have done if you'd wanted, but we liked working out in the fields and we shawed turnips and gathered the cabbages and different things and helped to get them all ready for market. So I think we did our own wee bit in our own way and it was very interesting, it was good fun, it was good fun and the chaps on the farm, who hadnae been called up yet, they were very helpful, very good. ... Mr Reid and his wife and his two sons, they were really, really gentlemen.

I had a horse called Nell, called her old Nell, and she wouldn't do as she was told at first, walking down from the field to the farm. ... And we usually walked up in a crowd anyway, 'cause when you went to do a job, there was girls, there was three girls, two girls and myself, and we walked up with the men, or the men were up there already, and we just got on with shawing and gathering in different things. ... We liked the harvest as well 'cause they brought the harvester [a threshing mill] in, and the first time when they said to me and Anne – that was the other girl – we went up and stood up on one side of this huge big opening and there was big wheels going round, what a noise they made, and that was the harvester. ... And you got a sheaf and you cut it, and there was a name for it, but I cannae mind the name, and you just picked up, they kept throwing up the sheaf and you cut the string and throwed it in and never thought of fallin' in or anything like that. ... And the laugh was the man that was running this was a wee man, the one that was putting, working the machinery on the top, he was a wee man, and he's sitting there, like that, and we looked quite big beside him because he was so tiny ... didnae expect a tiny man to be on such a big machine, a big harvester, so everything was more or less a laugh and a good time.

... You got your harvest rations, you didnae pay for anything, you got your food for the week to take back to the hostel or take it home, whatever. But we had Mrs Jimmy from the big house and she managed the Land Army house, the second house and it was beautiful. Everything was square, the rooms were square, the house was square, and it was just down from the big house, it was beautiful, we were well looked after. She was his cook and he had loaned her to the Land Army to help during the War 'cause they didnae have anybody to put in for to look after the Land Girls; and when we were in the hut in Humbie there were twelve of us, and then when we moved to the big house there was sixteen of us ... four in a bedroom, so we used to make our own fun at night. Someone had brought a gramophone, I think he had sent down a gramophone from the big house and we would spend all night dancing, if we werenae going anywhere, or play games, it was amazing the kinda games that you got to know [Ina laughs] and it was just all women. Lovely, I enjoyed my war, I can say that, I enjoyed my war. Lovely.

When you were doing the shawing, they just showed you how to quickly pull [the turnips] up, and use a knife for the roots and the top and drop them at the side. ... Then afterwards, after you'd done so many rows, if the men werenae coming round picking them up, sometimes you went round and helped them and put them into big boxes ... and then the lorry came along, a right old-fashioned trundling thing, you wondered how it went, you expected it to fall apart, but it did the job, it come round after you and picked up all the, if it was turnips or cabbages or if you were picking up leeks or anything, he came along behind you and got them all picked up. It was good fun, 'cause you had a good laugh when you were on the farm ... you had to go somewhere 'cause you were [called] up ... but it wasnae anything to be worried about just good fun!

I got to drive a tractor and it was lovely. It was a red one and it was called a Case – c ... a ... s ... e – and I used to drive that to the farm ... or if I was to take something up to the big fields.

I remember one day Mr Reid says I'll take you up to the top field and just you cut thorns – oh they were about this height – and he gave you this machine, this instrument, and there was a big knife on the end of it and it was so easy, you just went round like that and I thought, this is great, I'm helping the war effort. … And I was standing there and I heard a noise of a machine and he says to me don't worry about the planes going over, 'cause there was an airfield quite near hand I think, near Gifford, I'm no sure [probably East Fortune]. … But this time it was a black one and he came low down and I saw the yellow cross at the side and I thought, that's German, so I never moved, I never waved as I did to our own ones that were passing. … I just stood there and watched him and I thought he's coming awfully low, and I felt I was up on a hill but I just stood there with my machine, well my thingme, at the side of me, and he just came so far down and he just went on his way. If I'd lifted the instrument I think he might have thought it was a gun, hey? [laughs]

I didnae want to go [home] actually and there was quite a few of us and some of the girls didnae have a home – not a proper one – you know, they just went and moved about in the family, didnae seem to have any parents to look after them and they didnae want to go home. I didnae want to go home – I had parents and aunties and uncles and everything else – I didnae want to go home except at weekends, I really did like working on the farm.

Janet drove what they called the van but it was really what you would call a people carrier now, 'cause it held the two drivers and ten people. … And she said to me, 'Would you like to learn to drive', and I said, 'Oh yes, I would', and we got five shillings a week [laughs] for being a driver, which was something. Well, the wages were twenty-one shillings at first when we went in, and then they went up to twenty-three shillings, so to get the five shillings when you were driving, that was … [great].

… We didnae start working at six o'clock, we went an' got

them all drove right round, dropping everybody at their own farm, and then we got back to Highlea and I left Highlea after a while and went up to Upper Keith and that was really a gentleman, cannae mind what they would call it now, a gentleman farmer, he was a gentleman farmer and he dealt with all the, not just the ordinary, you know, it was more the sort of pedigree animals and cows and things like that – special pigs, there was a name for them. But oh, what a lovely man he was. There were two of us there at one time and we were taken in, no for elevenses … with the men, with their flasks and everything, but we were taken into the big house and had a lunch in the kitchen, huge big kitchen, and all the farm workers were in as well, you know, and it was lovely. You went in and you had your lunch and that was it, and if you didnae Mrs Jimmy gave you something away, your pack was there already, but we never needed it. … [The van] was very neat actually, it was just like a big car, but not as big as what you'd have thought it was to hold all the girls, you know. We were all nice and thin when we first went in and when we come out we were fat [laughs]. We were getting well fed. My mother says you're enjoying your war; I says yes, I am.

[I made] a lot of friends, I really did. … But we were finishing up in 1945 and the Colonel had wanted his house back, but there were quite a few of us, about six or seven and Mrs Gibson, she … I cannae remember the place where she stayed, was it in East Lothian? – certainly in the same area – and she said I'll have a word with him and see if he can let you stay on, 'cause I really wanted to stay and go home at the weekend, I didnae want to go back to the biscuit factory again. However, I thought that was all there was, but it wasnae, and he came back and he said I'll let you have it until such time as he gets organised and settled back into an ordinary life again, and we stayed another year and that was 1946.

The War finished 1945 and we stayed on till 1946 and then … Mrs Gibson came out and told us that he was closing it, he needed his house back again. I think his family was starting to come back from the War and that we'd have to go home, so that was it. And Mrs Gibson was killed – oh, what a lovely woman she was. She really was beautiful. She was in charge of all the Land Army and she was killed in an accident a few years after the War. We saw it in the paper – what a lovely woman she was, really a gentlewoman.

I'm sorry to say this, but we really enjoyed our war; it was different altogether to what we thought. My mother was fair worried. If you're away out on the land and no any houses, you won't be bothered with people bombing and things like that. The only thing we saw, they just went over. It was scary coming back to Edinburgh with running into our shelters and different things. Went home on a Saturday, finished at twelve on a Saturday and were back in the hostel on the quarter to eight bus to Gifford and then we were picked up and taken back to the hostel.

I loved the work as well too, nothing was too heavy. ... I remember, when I hadnae been there very long, some of them wore gloves, some of them didnae, and I had gloves, and when we were shawing on cold and frosty mornings, you know, and somebody says oh, I'm taking mine home, I'm taking mine back to the hostel, be about mid-morning, and I said no, I'm just going to stick mine on the hedge here, save putting them in my pocket, they were wet anyway – well, they were standing up like that [laughs] and next morning when I came out I couldnae get them off the hedge at all until it had thawed later on, it was useless. But it was funny just going in and seeing two hands just meeting you when you went in the gate.

We thoroughly enjoyed ourselves. And we used to go to Gifford for the pictures twice a week, Wednesday and Saturday, and if we werenae home for the weekend we piled into the car and we went to the pictures and went to the chip shop and got chips and ... and two small rolls. There'd be a dance on a Friday night, it was great! We thought we were going into the country and there wouldnae be anything, but there was plenty activity, more so than in the town. No, there was nothing in the town 'cause most had been shut down, but not where we were, we were alright. It was hard work, but you didnae look on it as hard work 'cause it was a lot of laughing and fun and things like that, and then you met some of the chaps on the farm at the dancing and things like that, so you were never short of partners, you know ... they were fair away with a Land Girl – oh, they're coming from the toon, they're toonies [laughs]. Seems daft now. It was good fun, it really was.

NOTES

1. National Archives of Scotland, NAS AF59.
2. Tyrer, N. *They Fought in the Fields. The Women's Land Army. The Story of a Forgotten Victory*, London, 1996, 1.
3. Clarke, G. *The Women's Land Army: A Portrait*. Bristol, 2008, 69.
4. Sackville-West, V. *The Women's Land Army*, London, 1944, 74.
5. NAS, AF59.
6. Tyrer, 1996, 49.
7. Tyrer, 1996, 60.
8. Sackville-West, 1944, 74.
9. Tyrer, 1996, 6.
10. The SWLA benevolent fund administered by the RSABI closed down in 2009.
11. NAS, AF59.
12. Northern Ireland did not have a Women's Land Army.
13. Tyrer, 1996, 38.
14. Sackville-West, 1944, 73.
15. An application form dated 2.4.1941, NAS 02024, AF59-247-00017.
16. Sackville-West, 1944, 74.
17. *Farming News and North British Agriculturist*, 19 January 1940.
18. Clarke, 2008, 89.
19. 'Bevin Boys' was the collective term used to describe men who had been conscripted to work in Britain's coalmines. They were named after Ernest Bevin, the Minister of Labour.
20. NAS AF59 – 247-00098.
21. De la Haye, A. Cinderellas in Breeches. In *Selvedge*, 32 (2010), 54-57.
22. <http:\\www.thelionspart.co.uk/liliesontheland/wla.html> [accessed March 2010]
23. National Archives of Scotland, NAS, AF59.
24. Strip grazing is a system of pasturage in which animals are given access to a fresh strip of pasture each day, with each strip being demarcated by use of an electric fence.
25. The Milk Marketing Board (MMB) was a government agency established in the 1930s to co-ordinate the production and distribution of milk. The MMB purchased all milk produced and sold it for liquid consumption or further processing. It then distri-buted the income to producers in proportion to the quantity of milk that they produced.
26. Sir Patrick Laird, at the time Secretary of the Department of Agriculture at the Scottish Office.
27. Under Secretary of State for Scotland.
28. Later Sir Norman Graham, who went on to become Secretary to the Scottish Education Depart-ment.
29. Chivas Farm was a farm owned by the jam-making firm.

GLOSSARY

This selective list contains only those terms found in the text that may need explanation:

basket whist, at a basket whist drive, typically the host at each table provided a 'basket' containing everything needed for the tea-break, such as best tablecloth and china, teapot and home-baking.

bothy, a basic dwelling for farm workers.

brock, food scraps; pig swill; rubbish.

cole, hay stack or rick.

discing, breaking-up of the earth in a ploughed field with a disc harrow.

firlot, equals 31 pints of barley, or 21 pints of wheat.

graip, a 3 or 4 pronged fork used for lifting dung or digging potatoes.

heuk, a reaping hook or sickle; simple hook.

hurkle, for cleaning between the drills. The drill harrow, or hurkle, has been used probably ever since husbandry was introduced.

lowsin' time, time to knock-off or finish work.

midser, a mid-morning snack.

nicky tams, pieces of string worn below the knee to keep the bottom of the trouser-leg lifted clear of the earth or dirt.

orrawoman, a farm labourer who does odd jobs on a farm.

reed, a cattle-yard; a bay.

roup, a sale by auction.

sowing sheet, a seed container – a piece of linen sometimes taut in a frame, held in front of the person sowing by hand – not to be confused with a sowing fiddle.

Snowcem, a white cement-based paint.

tumblin' tam, a horse draw implement to gather-up cut grass.

yokin' time, the act of yoking horses for work; hence more generally the commencement of a spell of work of any kind.